Million Dollar Habits

Proven Power Practices to Double and Triple Your Income

Brian Tracy

Entrepreneur®
Press

Editorial Director: Jere L. Calmes
Cover Design: Beth Hansen-Winter
Production and Composition: Eliot House Productions

This publication is designed to provide accurate and authoritative information in regard to the subject matter covered. It is sold with the understanding that the publisher is not engaged in rendering legal, accounting, or other professional services. If legal advice or other expert assistance is required, the services of a competent professional person should be sought.

Library of Congress Cataloging-in-Publication Data

Tracy, Brian.
    Million dollar habits: practical, proven power practices to double and triple your income/by Brian Tracy.
    p.   cm.
    ISBN 1-59918-029-4 (9781599180298 : alk. paper)
    1. Success in business. I. Title.
HF5386.T81423 2006
650.1'2—dc22   2006003285

Printed in Unites States

11 10 09   10 9 8 7 6 5

Table of Contents

You Are What You Do

Habit, my friend, is practice long pursued,
that at last becomes the man himself.
—EVENUS

*T*HANK YOU FOR READING THIS BOOK. IN the pages ahead, you are going to learn a proven and practical series of strategies and techniques that you can use to achieve greater success and happiness in every area of your life. I am going to share with you the so-called "secrets of success" practiced by most people who ever achieve anything worthwhile in life. When you learn and practice these techniques yourself, you will never be the same again.

THE GREAT QUESTION

Many years ago, I began asking the question "Why are some people more successful than others?" This question became the focal point of a lifelong search, taking me to more than 80 countries and through many thousands of books and articles on the subjects of philosophy, psychology, religion, metaphysics, history, economics, and business. Over time, the answers came to me, one by one, and gradually crystallized into a clear picture and a simple explanation:

You are where you are and what you are because of yourself. Everything you are today—or ever will be in the future—is up to you. Your life today is the sum total of your choices, decisions, and actions up to this point. You can create your own future by changing your behaviors. You can make new choices and decisions that are more consistent with the person you want to be and the things you want to accomplish with your life.

Just think! Everything that you are or ever will be is up to you. And the only real limit on what you can be, do, and have is the limit you place on your own imagination. You can take complete control of your destiny by taking complete control of your thoughts, words, and actions from this day forward.

THE POWER OF HABIT

Perhaps the most important discovery in the fields of psychology and success is that fully 95 percent of everything that you think, feel, do, and achieve is the result of habit. Beginning in childhood, you have developed a series of conditioned responses that lead you to react automatically and unthinkingly in almost every situation.

To put it simply, successful people have "success habits," and unsuccessful people do not. Successful, happy, healthy, prosperous men and women easily, automatically, and consistently do and say the right things in the right way at the right time. As a result, they accomplish 10 and 20 times more than average people who have not yet learned these habits or practiced these behaviors.

THE DEFINITION OF SUCCESS

Often people ask me to define the word *success*. My favorite definition is this:

> *Success is the ability to live your life the way you want to live it, doing what you most enjoy, surrounded by people you admire and respect.*

In a larger sense, success is the ability to achieve your dreams, desires, hopes, wishes, and goals in each of the important areas of your life.

Although each of us is unique and different from all other human beings who have ever lived, we all have four goals or desires in common. On a scale of one to ten, with one being the lowest and ten being the highest, you can conduct a quick evaluation of your life by giving yourself a grade in each of these four areas.

Healthy and Fit

The first goal common to all of us is *health and energy*. We all want to be healthy and fit, to have high levels of energy, and to live free of pain and illness. Today, with the incredible advances in medical science, the quality of our health and fitness and our lifespan are largely determined by design, not by chance. People with excellent health habits are far healthier, have more energy, and live longer and better than people with poor health habits. We will look at these habits and how we can develop them later in this book.

Excellent Relationships

The second goal we all have in common is to enjoy *excellent relationships*—intimate, personal, or social—with people we like and respect and who like, love, and respect us in turn. According to psychologist Sidney Jourard, fully 85 percent of your happiness will be determined by the quality of your relationships at each stage, and in each area, of your life. How well you get along with people and how much they like, love, and respect you has more impact on the quality of your life than perhaps any other factor. Throughout this book, you will learn the key habits of communication and behavior that build and maintain great relationships with other people.

Do What You Love

The third common goal is *to do work that we enjoy, to do it well, and to be well paid for it.* You want to be able to get and keep the job you want, to get paid more, and be promoted faster. You want to earn the very most that is possible for you at each stage of your career, whatever you do. In this book, you will learn how to develop the habits of the most successful and highest paid people in every field.

Achieve Financial Independence

The fourth goal we all have in common is to achieve financial independence. You want to reach the point in life where you have enough money so you never have to worry about money again. You want to be completely free of financial worries. You want to be able to order dinner in a restaurant without using the price listings to determine what you want to eat.

DEVELOPING "MILLION DOLLAR HABITS"

In the pages ahead, you will learn how to develop the "million dollar habits" of men and women who go from rags to riches in one generation. You will learn how to think more effectively, make better decisions, and take more effective actions than other people. You will learn how to organize your financial life in such a way that you achieve all your financial goals far faster than you imagine.

One of the most important goals you must achieve to be happy and successful in life is the development of your own character. You want to become an excellent person in every respect. You want to become the kind of person that others look up to and admire. You want to become a leader in your community and a role model for personal excellence to all the people around you.

The decisive factor in the achievement of character development and of the goals we all hold in common is the development of the specific habits that lead automatically and inevitably to the results you want to achieve.

ALL HABITS ARE LEARNED

The good news about habits is that all habits are learned as the result of practice and repetition. You can learn any habit you consider either necessary or desirable. By using your willpower and discipline, you can shape your personality and character in almost any way you desire. You can write the script of your own life, and if you are not happy with the current script, you can rip it up and write it again.

Just as your *good* habits are responsible for most of your success and happiness today, your bad habits are responsible for most of your problems and frustrations. But because bad habits are learned as well, they can be *unlearned* and replaced with good habits by the same process of practice and repetition.

First in Character

George Washington, the first president of the United States and the general in command of the Revolutionary Army, is rightly called "The Father of His Country." He was admired, if not worshiped, for the quality of his character, his graciousness of manner, and his correctness of behavior.

But that is not the way George Washington started off in life. He came from a middle-class family, with few advantages. One day, as a teenage boy aspiring to succeed and prosper, he came across a little book titled *The Rules of Civility and Decent Behavior in Company and Conversation*. Washington copied these 110 rules into a personal notebook. He carried it with him and reviewed them constantly throughout his life.

By practicing the "rules of civility," he developed the habits of behavior and manners that led to him being considered "first in the hearts of his countrymen." By deliberately practicing and repeating the habits that he most desired to make a part of his character, George Washington became in every respect a "self-made man." He learned the habits he needed to learn to become the kind of man he wanted to become.

The First Millionaire

During the same period, Benjamin Franklin, who began as a printer's apprentice and went on to become the first self-made millionaire in the American colonies, adapted a similar process of personal development.

As a young man, Benjamin Franklin felt that he was a little rough, ill mannered, and argumentative. He recognized that his attitudes and behaviors were creating animosity toward him from his associates and co-workers. He resolved to change by rewriting the script of his own personality.

He began by making up a list of 12 virtues that he felt the ideal person would possess. He then concentrated on the development of one virtue each week. All week long, as he went about his daily affairs, he would remind himself to practice that virtue, whether it was temperance, tolerance, or tranquility, on every occasion that it was called for. Over time, as he developed these virtues and made these habits a part of his character, he would practice one virtue for a period of two weeks, then three weeks, then one virtue per month.

Over time, he became one of the most popular personalities and statesmen of the age. He became enormously influential, both in Paris as an ambassador from the United States during the Revolutionary War and during the Constitutional Convention, when the Constitution and the Bill of Rights for the United States was debated, negotiated, and agreed upon. By working on himself to develop the habits of an excellent person, Franklin made himself into a person capable of shaping the course of history.

YOU ARE IN COMPLETE CONTROL

The fact is that good habits are hard to form but easy to live with. Bad habits, on the other hand, are easy to form, but hard to live with. In either case, you develop either good or bad habits as the result of your choices, decisions, and behaviors.

Writer and editor Horace Mann said, "Habits are like a cable. We weave a strand of it every day and soon it cannot be broken."

One of your great goals in life should be to develop the habits that lead to health, happiness, and true prosperity. Your aim should be to develop the habits of character that enable you to be the very best person you can imagine yourself becoming. The high purpose of your life should be to ingrain within yourself the habits that enable you to fulfill your full potential.

In the pages ahead, you will learn how your habit patterns are developed and how you can transform them in a positive way. You will learn how to become the kind of person who inevitably and relentlessly, like the waves of the ocean, moves onward and upward toward the accomplishment of every goal that you can set for yourself.

We first make our habits,
and then our habits make us.

—John Dryden

This book is dedicated to my three fine brothers—Robin, Dalmar, and Paul—each of them remarkable in his own way, each of them possessed of fine qualities, buttressed by great habits, and destined for wonderful things.

1

Where Your Habits Begin

> Any act often repeated soon forms a habit; and habit allowed, steadily gains in strength. At first it may be as a spider's web, easily broken through, but if not resisted, it soon binds us with chains of steel."
>
> —TRYON EDWARDS

*Y*OU ARE EXTRAORDINARY! YOU CAME into this world with more talents and abilities than you could ever use. You could not exhaust your full potential if you lived 100 lifetimes.

Your amazing brain has 20 billion cells, each of which is connected to as many as 20,000 other cells. The possible combinations and permutations of ideas, thoughts, and insights that you can generate are equivalent to the number one followed by eight pages of zeros. According to brain expert Tony Buzan, this number is greater than all the molecules in the known universe. Whatever you have accomplished in life to this date is only a small fraction of what you are truly capable of achieving.

The psychologist Abraham Maslow once wrote, "The story of the human race is the story of men and women selling themselves short." The average person settles for far less than he or she is truly capable of achieving. Compared with what you could do, everything you have accomplished so far is only a small part of what is truly possible for you.

The challenge is that you come into the world with the most incredible brain, surrounded by unlimited possibilities for success, happiness, and achievement, but you start off with *no instruction manual.* As a result, you have to figure it all out for yourself. Most people never do. They go through life doing the very best they can, but they never come within shouting distance of doing, having, and being all that is possible for them.

COMING FROM BEHIND

I started off in life with few advantages. My father was not always employed, and my family never seemed to have any money. I began working and paying for my own clothes and expenses when I was 10 years old, doing odd jobs around the neighborhood. I hoed weeds, delivered newspapers, mowed lawns, and raked leaves. When I was old enough, I got a job washing dishes in the back of a small hotel. My biggest promotion at that time was moving to washing pots and pans.

I left high school without graduating and worked at laboring jobs for several years. I worked in sawmills stacking lumber and in the woods slashing brush with a chain saw. I dug ditches and wells. I worked on farms and ranches. I worked in factories and on construction sites. For a time, I was a galley boy on a Norwegian freighter in the North Atlantic. I earned my living by the sweat of my brow.

When I could no longer find a laboring job, I got a job in straight commission sales, cold calling from door to door and office to office. For a long time, I was one sale away from homelessness. If I did not make a sale that day and get my commission immediately so I could pay for my room at the boarding house, I would have been out on the street. This was not a great way to live.

THE KEY TO SUCCESS

Then one day I began asking that question, "Why is it that some people are more successful than others?" Especially, "Why is it that some salespeople are more successful than others?"

Looking for an answer to that one question, I did something that changed my life and began the formation of a habit that profoundly affected my future. I went and *asked* the most successful salesman in my company what he was doing differently than I was. And he told me. And I did what he told me to do. And my sales went up.

In the Bible it says, "Ask and ye shall receive." I soon developed the habit of asking everyone, in every way possible, for the answers that I needed to move ahead more rapidly. I began to read books on selling and put into action what I learned. I listened to audio programs while I walked and, eventually, as I drove around. I attended every sales seminar I could find. I continually asked other successful salespeople for advice. And I developed the habit of immediately taking action on any advice or good idea that I received or learned.

As a result, and not surprisingly, my sales went up and up, and eventually I surpassed everyone in my company. Soon my company made me a sales manager and asked me to teach other people what enabled me to be so successful. Soon I was recruiting people with newspaper ads, teaching them the sales methods and techniques that I had learned, and sending them out to call on prospects and customers. In no time at all, my students were making sales and moving upward and onward in their own lives. Many of those early salespeople are millionaires today.

THE IRON LAW OF THE UNIVERSE

What I learned from this experience was the great Law of Cause and Effect. This is the foundational principle of Western philosophy and of modern thought. It says that for every cause, there is an effect. Everything happens for a reason. Nothing happens by accident. This law says that even if you do not know the reason why something happens, there is still a reason that explains it.

Here is one of the most important of all success principles: If you do what other successful people do, you will eventually get the same results that they do. And if you don't, you won't.

Nature is neutral. Nature does not favor one person over another. The Bible says, "God makes the rain to fall on the just and the unjust." When you do the things that other successful people do, over and over again, you will eventually get the same results that they do. It is not a matter of luck, or chance, or accident. It is a matter of law.

This was an extraordinary idea for me. Even today I am awed by the immensity and power of this simple principle. If you want to be happy, healthy, prosperous, popular, positive, and confident, just find out how other people who are enjoying these benefits got that way and do the same things that they do. Think the same thoughts. Feel the same feelings. Take the same actions. And as sure as two plus two makes four, you will eventually get the same results as others do. It is no miracle.

YOU CAN LEARN ANYTHING

Over the years, I have worked in a variety of businesses and industries. I have traveled in 90 countries, learned different languages, and developed various skills. In my 30s, I completed high school and got a business degree from a leading university. In every job and in every situation, I started off by asking, "What are the rules or principles for success in this area of activity?" I then read books, attended courses, and asked everyone I could find for their insights and ideas.

When I became a sales manager, I read every book and article I could find on sales management, and applied the ideas and principles to building and directing a successful sales force. When I got into real estate development, I read dozens of books on the subject. Within a year, starting with no money and no contacts, I developed and built a $3 million shopping center and came out owning 25 percent of it.

When I got into the importation and distribution of Japanese automobiles, I again read the books, spoke to the experts, and did my research to find out how to set up a network of dealerships. In the next four years, I established 65 dealerships and imported and sold more than $25 million worth of vehicles.

Over the past 22 years, in my work with more than 500 corporations, my entire focus has been on discovering the reasons for sales, revenues, and profits in each business or industry and then determining how those principles could be best utilized to achieve the results of the most successful companies.

When people complimented me on my successes, I eagerly shared with them what I had learned in each area. I told them that they too could learn anything that they needed to learn to achieve any goal they could set for themselves. All they had to do was to find out the cause-and-effect relationships in any area of endeavor and then apply them to their own activities. If they did this, they would soon get the same results as other successful people, I told them.

TAKING CONTROL OF YOUR LIFE

But instead of taking this advice, they would nod, smile, and agree and then turn away and go about their day-to-day business. They would start work at the last possible moment, waste much of the day in idle conversation with co-workers and personal business, leave work at the earliest possible time, and then spend their evenings socializing or watching television.

In frustration, I began to study psychology and metaphysics. I eventually learned that there are a series of universal principles and timeless truths that explain much of human success and failure. These principles explain happiness and unhappiness, riches and poverty, health and ill health, and good and poor relationships. These mental laws explain why some people have wonderful lives and why others do not.

The Law of Control

The first law that I discovered was the Law of Control. This law says that "You feel happy to the degree to which you feel you are in control of your own life. You feel unhappy to the degree to which you feel you are not in control of your own life."

Modern psychology calls this "locus of control theory." Psychologists differentiate between an internal locus of control and an external locus of control. Your locus of control is where you feel the control exists in each area of your life. This location determines your happiness or unhappiness more than any other factor.

For example, if you feel that you are the primary creative force in your own life, that you make your own decisions, and that everything that happens to you is a result of yourself and your own behaviors, you have a solid internal locus of control. As a result, you will feel strong, confident, and happy. You will think with greater clarity and perform at higher levels than the average person.

On the other hand, if you feel that your life is controlled by other factors or people—by your job, your boss, your childhood experiences, your bills, your health, your family, or anything else—you have an *external* locus of control. You will feel like a victim. You will feel like a pawn in the hands of fate. You will soon develop what Dr. Martin Seligman of the University of Pennsylvania calls "learned helplessness." You will feel helpless and unable to change or improve your situation. You will soon develop the habit of blaming others and making excuses for your problems. This type of thinking leads inevitably to anger, frustration, and failure. We will talk more about this later in this chapter.

The Power of Belief

The next law I discovered was the Law of Belief. This is the basic principle that underlies most religion, psychology, philosophy, and metaphysics. The law of belief says that, "Whatever you believe, with conviction, becomes your reality."

In the New Testament, Jesus says, "According to your faith, it is done unto you." In the Old Testament, it says, "As a man thinketh, in his heart (his beliefs), so is he." Professor William James of Harvard wrote in 1905, "Belief creates the actual fact."

The fact is, you do not believe what you see, but rather, you see what you already believe. Your deeply held beliefs form a screen of prejudices that distort your external reality and cause you to see things not the way *they* are, but the way *you* are.

The worst of all beliefs is *self-limiting beliefs*. These are beliefs that you have developed through life, usually false, that cause you to believe you are limited in some way. Your negative beliefs soon become habitual ways of thinking. You may believe you lack intelligence, creativity, personality, the ability to speak publicly, the ability to earn a high income, the ability to lose weight, or the ability to achieve your goals. As a result of your self-limiting beliefs, you continually "sell yourself short," give up easily in the pursuit of a goal—and even worse—tell other people around you that you lack certain qualities or abilities. Your beliefs then become your realities. "You are not what you think you are, but what you *think*, you are."

In developing million dollar habits, one of the most important steps you take is to challenge your self-limiting beliefs. You begin this process by imagining that you have no limitations at all. When you develop your mind to the point where you absolutely believe that you can do anything you put your mind to, you will find a way to make that belief a reality. As a result, your whole life will change.

As we will discuss later, beliefs are the hardest things of all to change. But there is good news: all beliefs are *learned*. And anything that has been learned can be *unlearned*. You can develop the beliefs of courage, confidence, and unstoppable persistence that you need for great success by reprogramming your subconscious mind in a specific way.

Your Self-Fulfilling Prophecies

The next law I discovered was the Law of Expectations. This law says, "Whatever you expect, with confidence, becomes your own self-fulfilling prophecy." In other words, you do not necessarily get what you want, but rather what you expect.

If you confidently expect something to happen, this expectation has a powerful effect on your attitude and your personality. The more confident your expectations, the more likely it is that you will do and say the things that are consistent with what you expect to happen. As a result, you will dramatically increase the probabilities that you will achieve exactly what you are hoping for.

One of the wonderful things about expectations is that you can manufacture your own. You can get up each morning and say, "I believe something wonderful is going to happen to me today." As you go through the day, you create a force field of expectations that surrounds you and affects the people with whom you come in contact. And in some remarkable way, a series of wonderful things, both large and small, will happen to you throughout the day.

Successful people expect—in advance—to be successful. Happy people expect to be happy. Popular people expect to be liked by others. They develop the habit of expecting that something good will happen in every situation. They expect to benefit from every occurrence, even temporary setbacks and failures. They expect the best of other people and always assume the best of intentions. And they are seldom disappointed.

The flip side of positive expectations are the negative expectations many people have. Unhappy people expect to fail more often than they succeed. They expect that other people will hurt or disappoint them. They expect their ventures to do poorly. Instead of expecting the best, they expect the worst, and because the law is neutral, they are seldom disappointed.

One of the most important things you can do to assure a happy, healthy, prosperous life is to expect the very best from every person or situation, no matter how it may look at the moment. Develop the habit of positive expectations. You will be amazed at the effect this has on you and on the people around you.

You Are a Living Magnet

The next law I learned about was the Law of Attraction. This law says, "You are a living magnet; you invariably attract into your life the people, ideas, and circumstances that harmonize with your dominant thoughts."

This law of attraction has been written and spoken about for 5,000 years. It is one of the most important of all principles in explaining success and failure. The law of attraction says your thoughts are activated by your emotions, either positive or negative, and that they then create a force field of energy around you that attracts into your life, like iron filings to a magnet, exactly the people and circumstances that are in harmony with those thoughts.

Like all mental laws, the law of attraction is neutral. If you think positive thoughts, you attract positive people and circumstances. If you think negative thoughts, you attract negative people and circumstances. Successful, happy people continually think and talk about what they want to attract into their lives. Unsuccessful, unhappy people are continually talking about the people and situations that cause them to feel angry and frustrated.

One of the most important habits you can develop is the habit of keeping your mind full of exciting, positive, emotionalized pictures and images of the exact things you want to see materialize in your life and in the world around you. This is one of the most difficult of disciplines, but one that pays off in extraordinary ways.

As Within, So Without

The summary law of the laws we have just discussed is the Law of Correspondence. This law says, "Your outer world is a reflection of your inner world."

It is as though you live in a 360-degree mirror. Everywhere you look, you see yourself reflected back at you. People treat you the way you treat them. The way you think about your physical body will be reflected in your health habits and your appearance. The way you think about people and your relationships will be reflected back to you in the quality of your friendships and your family life. The way you think about success and prosperity will be reflected in the results that you enjoy in your career and your material life. In every case, your outer world reflects back to you, like a mirror image, exactly what you are thinking in the deepest recesses of your mind.

When you put the Laws of Cause and Effect, Control, Belief, Expectations, Attraction, and Correspondence together, you arrive at the great universal principle that explains your life and everything that happens to you: *"You become what you think about—most of the time."*

Just think! You become what you think about most of the time. You always move in the direction of your dominant thoughts. Everything in your outer world is controlled and determined by what you are thinking in your inner world.

The good news is that there is only one thing in the universe over which you have complete control, and that is the content of your conscious mind. Only you can decide what you think about most of the time. And fortunately, this is all the control that you need to shape your own life and determine your own future. By taking complete control of your conscious thoughts, you can control the direction of your life. By taking control, you will feel happy, powerful, confident, and free. You will become unstoppable.

Action Exercises

$ Look at your field today. Identify the three most important reasons why some people are more successful than others.

$ Accept complete responsibility for your life and everything that happens to you; refuse to make excuses or to blame others for anything.

$ What self-limiting beliefs do you have that might be holding you back? What if they weren't true at all?

$ Expect the best of yourself and others. What would you change if you were absolutely guaranteed of success?

$ In what ways have your dominant thoughts and emotions attracted people, circumstances, and situations into your life? How could you change this?

$ Everywhere you look, there you are. What do you need to change in your inner world if you want to see changes in your outer world?

$ Determine the three most important habits of thought, about yourself and others, that you could develop to be happier and more successful.

You can do anything you think you can. This knowledge is literally the gift of the gods, for through it you can solve every human problem. It should make of you an incurable optimist. It is the open door to unlimited possibilities."

—ROBERT COLLIER

2

The Master Program of Success

> The whole secret of a successful life is
> to find out what it is one's destiny to do,
> and then do it.
>
> —HENRY FORD

*T*HE GREAT QUESTION FOR SUCCESS IS this: what do you think about most of the time? Why is it that some people think positive, constructive, and success-oriented thoughts while others think negative, pessimistic thoughts that lead inevitably to failure and underachievement?

Many successful people over the years have been asked, "What do you think about, most of the time?" Their answers are simple and consistent and yet so profound that they can be life changing. In short, successful people most of the time think about what they *want* and how to get that.

Unsuccessful people, on the other hand, most of the time think and talk about what they *don't want* and *who is to blame* for their problems and difficulties. As a result, they attract more and more of what they don't want and what makes them unhappy into their lives. The laws are neutral. Whatever you think and talk about most of the time eventually comes into your life.

For more than 100 years, psychologists have worked to understand and explain the functioning of the human mind. Starting with Sigmund Freud and continuing through Alfred Adler, Karl Jung, Abraham Maslow, William Glasser, Eric Fromm, B. F. Skinner to the present day, psychologists have sought the reasons for happiness and unhappiness, success and failure, achievement and underachievement. They have all concluded, in one way or another, how your mind is programmed in early childhood plays a decisive role in almost everything you think, feel, and accomplish as an adult.

YOUR MASTER PROGRAM

I have personally read hundreds of books and thousands of articles on psychology and the functioning of the human mind. Perhaps the most significant discovery for me was learning about the role of the *self-concept* in human performance and behavior. Margaret Meade, the anthropologist, called the idea of self-concept, "the most important breakthrough in the understanding of human potential in the 20th century."

Your self-concept is the "master program" of your subconscious computer. It acts as your mental operating system. Every thought, feeling, emotion, experience, and decision you have ever had is permanently recorded on this mental hard drive. Once recorded, these impressions then influence the way you think, feel, and behave from that point onward.

Your self-concept precedes and predicts your levels of effectiveness in every area of your life. You always act on the outside in a manner consistent with the way you feel and think about yourself on the inside. Your self-concept explains why the mental laws have such an inordinate effect on your personality.

The Role of the Mini-Self-Concept

Once your self-concept in a particular area is formed, you always act in a manner consistent with it. You may have extraordinary ability in a particular area, but if your self-concept is poor in that area, you will always perform below your true potential.

It turns out you have a "mini-self-concept" for every area of your life that you consider important. For example, you have a self-concept for how creative you are. You have a self-concept for how well you speak in public, for your memory, and for your ability to learn new subjects. You have a self-concept for how popular you are and how well you get along with other people. You have a self-concept for what kind of a spouse or partner you are and how desirable or attractive you are to members of the opposite sex. You have a self-concept for what kind of a parent you are. You have a self-concept for how well you perform in each sport or physical activity. You have a self-concept for how organized or disorganized you are, how well you manage your time, how productive you are, and how much you get done in an average day. You have a self-concept for your ability to read, write, and do mathematics.

In your business and career, in the context of million-dollar habits, you have a self-concept for every aspect of your financial life. You have a self-concept for how much you earn and how hard you have to work to earn that amount of money. You have a self-concept for how rapidly you are promoted and how much your earnings increase month by month and year by year.

You have a self-concept for how much you earn on an annual basis and for how much you will be earning in the future. You have a self-concept for how well you save, invest, spend, and accumulate money. You have a self-concept of your personal financial net worth and how much you are able to acquire in the months and years of your life. Every aspect of your financial life on the outside is determined by your self-concept on the inside relative to that way of dealing with money.

Your Comfort Zone

Whatever your self-concept, your habit of thinking with regard to money or any other area of performance very soon becomes your "comfort zone." Your comfort zone then becomes your greatest single obstacle to improved performance. Once you get into a comfort zone in any area, you will strive and struggle unconsciously to remain in that comfort zone, even though it may be vastly below what you are truly capable of achieving in that area.

For example, with regard to money, if your comfort zone is earning $50,000 per year, that is how much you will earn. No matter what happens in the world around you, recessions, depressions, booms, and busts, you will eventually stabilize at an earning level of $50,000 per year. You will use all your talents and abilities to get into and maintain that financial comfort zone.

If you are accustomed to earning $100,000 per year and you lose your job or move across the country and start over, within a few months, you will be earning $100,000 per year. Once your self-concept level of income is developed and permanently programmed into your mental hard drive as a habit, your subconscious and superconscious minds will always find a way to achieve that level of income, no matter what happens around you.

The key to achieving your full potential, to increasing your income to vastly higher levels than it is today, and to enjoying the very best that is possible for you in every area of life is for you to raise your self-concept in that area. You must develop new habits of thinking about what is possible for you. The way you accomplish vastly more on the outside is by changing your thoughts and feelings about your potential in that area on the inside.

REPROGRAM YOURSELF FOR GREATER SUCCESS

In medicine it is said that "proper diagnosis is half the cure." To that end, let us look at the three parts of your self-concept, how they interact with each other, and how you can act to alter or improve them in any way you want.

Your Ideal Self

⌐TD
⌐ısıon

The first part of your self-concept is your *self-ideal*. This is the ideal image or picture you have of yourself, as if you were already the very best person you could possibly be. Your self-ideal is made up of your wishes, hopes, dreams, goals, and fantasies about your perfect future life, combined with the qualities and virtues that you admire most in yourself and in other people. Your self-ideal is a composite of the very best person you could imagine yourself being, living the very best life you could possibly live.

High-performing, successful, happy people have very clear self-ideals. They have clear ideas of what they like, respect, and admire. They have clear ideas about the virtues, values, and attributes of the superior men and women they want to emulate. The most successful people have an uplifting, inspiring vision of what a truly excellent person looks like and how he or she behaves.

Because of the Law of Attraction, you inevitably move in the direction of becoming that which you most admire. The greater clarity you have with regard to the ideal future life you want to live and the ideal person you want to be, the faster you will move toward becoming that person and the more opportunities will open up for you to make your ideal future vision a reality.

DEVELOP POSITIVE ROLE MODELS

In one study conducted some years ago, the researchers found many men and women who accomplished great things had—when they were young—been avid readers of the biographies and autobiographies of successful people. It seems you have a natural tendency to identify with the hero or heroine in any story you read, watch, or hear. When you continually immerse your mind in the stories of men and women who have accomplished wonderful things with their lives, you unconsciously identify with those characters and actually absorb their values, virtues, and qualities into your own personality.

Dr. David McClelland, a Harvard professor, in his book *The Achieving Society* (Free Press, 1985), explains how role models have an inordinate effect on shaping the character and personality of the young. One of his conclusions was that the men and women who are the most admired and held up as models in society during the formative years of a young person have an inordinate influence on the character and aspirations of that person when he or she grows to adulthood.

By the same token, young people who have positive role models around them when they are growing up are much more likely to become men and women of quality and character as adults than young people who have no role models, or even worse, negative role models as often occurs today.

With regard to the self-ideal, unhappy, unsuccessful men and women tend to be very fuzzy or unclear about their ideals. If you ask them what they consider to be the most valuable and important qualities in human character and personality, they have either unclear or contradictory answers. This lack of clarity or certainty about what constitutes an ideal person often causes an individual to go around in circles in life, to associate with negative influences, and spend time with people who are equally unclear and unfocused about "the person they want to be when they grow up."

YOUR VALUES SHAPE YOUR PERSONALITY

The values you choose to live by, and the way you define those values, shape and influence your personality and your achievements as much or more than any other single factor. When you take the time to think through and develop absolute clarity about the key values and qualities you admire the most and wish the most to incorporate into yourself, you begin to shape and direct your whole personality and determine the results you achieve in the future.

As you think about your values and reflect upon how you could incorporate them into your life and behaviors, you become a different person. As a result, you attract different people and opportunities into your life. Your outer world soon begins to mirror your inner world. You start to move more rapidly toward the achievement of your most important goals, and your goals begin to move rapidly toward you. It all begins with you taking complete control of the formation and development of your personal self-ideal.

How You See Yourself

The second part of your self-concept is your *self-image*. Beginning with the work of Dr. Maxwell Maltz and his book *Psycho-Cybernetics* (Free Press, 1985), we learn that the way you see yourself on the inside largely determines how you perform on the outside.

If you see yourself as positive, popular, productive, and successful on the inside, that is exactly how you will act on the outside. The way you behave on the outside will largely determine the results you get. The results you get will reinforce your self-image, in either a positive or negative way, and will set you up to repeat the same behaviors in the next similar situation.

Your self-image is often called your "inner mirror." This is the mirror that you look into prior to engaging in any performance or entering into any event of importance. If you see yourself as confident and successful prior to meeting a new person, applying for a job, or making a presentation, that is how you will perform in the actual situation. If you have a poor self-image, if you see yourself as not being particularly popular, confident, or attractive, your negative self-image will cause you to feel clumsy, awkward, and inadequate in subsequent situations.

One of the most important habits you can develop is the habit of feeding your mind before every important situation with positive pictures and images of yourself performing at your very best. Take a few moments, as athletes, politicians, and performers do, and imagine yourself as if you were outstanding at what you were about to do. Hold that picture in your mind for as long as you possibly can. Then, relax and let it go. Later, when you find yourself in that situation, your subconscious mind will remember the picture and give you the words, actions, and gestures that correspond exactly to the picture you created a short time before.

The Core of Your Personality

The third part of your self-concept is your *self-esteem*. This is the feeling or emotional component of your personality, the "reactor core" of your subconscious mind. Your level of self-esteem determines the vitality and energy of your personality and is the control valve on your performance.

Many psychologists today agree that your level of self-esteem is the most important part of your personality and largely predicts your success or failure, happiness or unhappiness, in every area of your life. In fact, your self-esteem is so important that you tend to organize your whole life around it. Almost everything you do is either to gain self-esteem or to protect against the loss of self-esteem.

The rule with regard to your self-esteem is that "everything counts!" Everything that happens to you and around you affects your self-esteem in some way. Everything either increases your self-esteem or lowers it. Everything that happens to you either supports your self-esteem or threatens it. You are like the proverbial "long tailed cat in a room full of rocking chairs." Every word or gesture of other people toward you affects your self-esteem in some way. The preservation and development of your self-esteem thus becomes the key to high performance, happiness, and great success.

COMPARING YOUR BEHAVIOR WITH YOUR IDEAL

Your self-esteem is affected by many factors. One of the most important is the distance between your self-image, the way you see yourself in the moment, and your self-ideal, the way you would ideally like to be sometime in the future.

Whenever you feel your current performance and behavior is consistent with the best person that you can possibly be, your self-esteem goes up. You feel happier and more exhilarated. You have more energy and enthusiasm. You are more positive and personable with others.

On the other hand, whenever your current performance or behavior seems to be inconsistent or distant from the person that you would most like to be, your self-esteem goes down. You feel anxious and unhappy. You feel self-conscious and embarrassed. You feel frustrated and angry.

The good news is that the greater clarity you have with regard to your self-ideal—the person you would most like to be—the easier it is for you to tailor your performance and behavior to be consistent with the kind of person you most admire. And every time you do or say anything that you feel is more consistent with the best person you can possibly be, your self-esteem goes up. You feel happier and more confident. You feel more positive and powerful. You feel capable of doing more and better things in that area and in other areas of your life.

THE BEST DEFINITION OF SELF-ESTEEM

The very best definition of self-esteem is "how much you like yourself." What we have found is that, the more you like yourself, the better you do. And the better you do, the more you like yourself. Each time you perform well in any area, your self-esteem goes up. You like yourself more, and you perform even better in that area and in other areas as well.

The most powerful words you can use to take control of your personality and build your self-esteem are *"I like myself!"* The more you repeat the words "I like myself!" to yourself, the happier and more confident you feel and the better you perform in whatever you are doing.

When I first learned this powerful affirmation many years ago, my self-esteem was quite low. I had a poor self-image. I had a vague self-ideal. I was plagued by fears and doubts and tended to compare myself in negative terms with other people. To counter these feelings, I began to repeat the words, "I like myself!" 10, 20, and even 50 times a day. It had a remarkable impact on my personality.

Perhaps the most powerful words in your vocabulary are the words you say to yourself and believe. Most psychologists say that fully 95 percent of your emotions are determined by the words that are running through your mind at any given time. And your mind is very much like a vacuum: it does not remain empty for very long. If you do not deliberately fill your mind with positive, constructive words, it will fill up by itself with your fears, worries, and concerns.

To put it another way, if you do not deliberately plant flowers in the garden of your mind, weeds will grow automatically, with no encouragement or support.

POSITIVE SELF-TALK SHAPES YOUR PERSONALITY

One of the most important habits you can develop is the habit of talking to yourself positively most of the time. And the most positive words that you can use throughout the day, especially prior to any event of importance or significance, are the words "I like myself!" You cannot say these words to yourself without feeling happier, especially if you repeat them emotionally and emphatically,

Every time you say "I like myself!" your self-esteem goes up. As your self-esteem increases, you feel more positive and optimistic. You become eager to set bigger goals and face greater challenges. The more you like yourself, the greater courage and confidence you have. The more you like yourself, the less your fears and doubts get in your way or interfere with your success. And you get all the benefits of self-esteem enhancement by continually repeating "I like myself!"

SUPERCHARGE YOUR PERSONALITY

The higher your self-esteem, the faster and easier it is for you to develop the million-dollar habits that enable you to accomplish extraordinary things with your life. Since everything you do on the outside is controlled by your subconscious mind—your current programming—as you change your self-concept, you change your reality.

Your self-concept is the seat of the Laws of Belief, Expectation, Attraction, and Correspondence. Your self-concept determines what you think about most of the time. Your self-concept contains the roots of learned helplessness. Your self-concept represents your comfort zone. Your main goal is to take complete control over the evolution and development of your self-concept and shape your personality and your character into an extraordinary person who can accomplish remarkable things.

Take time to become absolutely clear about the virtues, values, qualities, and attributes that you most admire and most aspire to make a part of your personality. Prior to every event of importance, create a clear mental picture of yourself performing at your very best, consistent with the highest values and qualities that you have or desire to have.

Especially, continually repeat the magic words "I like myself!" over and over again, until they are accepted by your subconscious mind and become a permanent part of your personality. The more you like and respect yourself and consider yourself to be a valuable and important person, the faster you will develop every other habit, quality, and attribute that you need to fulfill your full potential.

THE FOUNDATION OF YOUR PERSONALITY

At this point, many people ask, "Where does your self-concept come from? How does it begin? How does it develop? What are the major influences that shape your self-concept and how can you change your self-concept once it has developed?" These are vital questions, and there are definite answers for them.

Most psychologists believe that each child is born with no self-concept at all. Every thought, feeling, idea, opinion, belief, or conviction that you have as an adult has been learned, starting in early infancy. You have been taught to believe the things you believe by the people and influences around you over the course of your lifetime, especially when you were a child.

It is true that each child is born with certain personality character-istics, propensities, talents, leanings, and other unique attributes and qualities. Some psychologists say that fully 60 percent of personality characteristics, such as courage, extroversion, musical interest, sensitivity, athletic ability, and so on, are inborn and innate. This is why children born into the same family, with the same parents and similar upbringing, often turn out totally different from each other. But in terms of self-concept, how a person thinks and feels about themselves relative to their ability and potential, this is learned from early infancy.

Your Two Natural Qualities

When you are born, you come into the world with two natural qualities. First, you are completely *unafraid.* You are totally fearless. You have no rea-son to be afraid because you have had no experiences to make you afraid. The second natural quality is that you are completely *spontaneous.* You laugh, cry, pee, poop, sleep, and express yourself with no thought or con-cern about whether anybody approves or disapproves. These are your nat-ural qualities in a state of nature.

As an adult, when you feel completely relaxed and safe, surrounded by people you like and trust, your natural tendency is to revert to being completely open and unafraid, spontaneous and expressive. This is the ideal condition of the completely happy, fully functioning adult.

Starting early in childhood, as the result of the things your parents do and say, you begin to learn the two basic negative habit patterns that then become the most destructive influences in your life as an adult.

The first negative habit pattern that you learn is called the inhibitive negative habit pattern. This is what soon becomes the fear of failure, risk, and loss. As a child, your natural urge is to explore your environment. You eagerly reach out to touch, taste, feel, and experiment with everything around you. But often your parents react and even overreact to this behavior by discouraging you as much as possible. They say, "No! Get away from that! Don't touch that! Leave that alone!" Many parents reinforce their words and threats with spankings and punishment.

Children need love like roses need rain. Love is as important to the developing child as is food. Any interruption of the flow of unconditional love to the child causes the child to feel nervous and frightened. Some psychologists say virtually all adult problems are rooted in the phenomena of "love withheld" in early childhood.

When your parents become angry with you as the result of your natural desire and drive to explore your world and your environment, you have no way of understanding that this is because they fear for your safety. Instead, as a child, you merely react and respond with the idea that "Every time I try or touch or taste something new or different, my mother or father gets angry at me. It must be because I am incapable and incompetent. It must be because I am no good. It must be because *I can't do it*."

FEAR OF TRYING ANYTHING NEW

This feeling of "I can't" begins the development of the fear of failure. If you are discouraged or punished too often as a child, very early in life you will become fearful of trying new things. This fear will then carry over into later childhood, adolescence, and adult life. Thereafter, whenever you think of doing something new or different, something that entails risk or uncertainty, your first reaction will be "I can't!" As soon as you say the words "I can't" to yourself, you will begin immediately to think of all the reasons why such a thing is not possible for you. You will think and talk in terms of failure, rather than success. You will think of the uncertainties and all the possible risks that may occur. Before you even try something new, you will talk yourself out of it.

Napoleon Hill, author of *Think and Grow Rich* (Fawcett Books, 1990), once asked an audience, "What is the average number of times that a person tries to achieve a new goal before they give up?" After several guesses from the audience, he gave the answer. "Less than one."

The point he made was that most people give up before they try the first time. They give up without trying even once. Even though they want to improve their lives, increase their incomes, and accomplish more than they do today, as soon as the new goal pops into their mind, most people automatically respond with the words "I can't!" And then they begin thinking of all the reasons why it is not possible for them.

The most important habit you can develop for great happiness and success is the habit of repeating to yourself and believing "I can do anything I put my mind to!"

The most powerful words that you can repeat, over and over, to neutralize and overcome the fear of failure, are *"I can do it! I can do it!"*

The kindest words a parent can tell his or her child, in addition to "I love you," are the words "You can do anything that you set your mind to." It is amazing how many people's lives have been dramatically affected by the influence of a single person, a parent, relative, or friend, who simply told them, over and over again, "*You can do it.*"

What Others Might Say

The second negative habit pattern we learn is the compulsive negative habit pattern. This creates the fear of rejection or criticism. We are all sensitive to the opinions of others, especially to the opinions and reactions of our parents when we are growing up. Parents often take advantage of their children's need to please to control and manipulate them. They give or withhold approval and support based on the behavior of the child at the moment.

When the child does or says something the parents don't like, they immediately become rejecting and critical of the child. Since the approval and support of the parent is like a psychological lifeline to the emotional health of the child, the child is immediately affected and pulls back from the behavior in order to regain the love and approval of the parents.

Parents very soon slip into the habit of manipulating the child with "carrot and stick" treatment. They alternate with approval and disapproval, with compliments and criticism, to control and manipulate the child's behavior.

As a child, you are too young to understand what is going on. You know only one thing. The love and approval of your parents is indispensable to your well-being. It is the key to your emotional health. You therefore learn that "If I want to get along, I go along." At an early age, you begin to conform your behaviors to earn the approval, and avoid the disapproval, of your parents.

The Approval of Others

As you grow older, you become increasingly sensitive to the approval or disapproval of others, starting with members of your family and then progressing to your friends and associates. Teenagers, especially, become extremely sensitive to whether they are liked or disliked by their peers. Instead of being fearless and spontaneous, completely open, honest, and expressive, they begin to shape their behaviors to conform with whatever they feel their peers will approve of at the moment.

The child does not know why the parent is behaving this way. The child simply concludes that, "Every time I do something that Mommy or Daddy disapproves of, they stop loving me. Therefore, whatever it is, I have to do what makes them happy. I have to do what pleases them. I have to do what they want if I want to be safe."

These fears are often manifested in the words "I have to!" As an adult, the child who was subjected to disapproval and destructive criticism becomes hypersensitive to the attitudes and opinions of others. They are continually saying, "I have to do this" or "I have to do that." When the fear of rejection becomes extreme, the individual becomes so hypersensitive to the opinions of others that he or she cannot make a decision until absolutely convinced that everyone in the immediate world will approve and support the decision.

Like a Deer in the Headlights

The worst situation of all, which is quite common in most people, is the combined feeling of "I have to" but "I can't." People feel that they have to do something in order to win the approval of an important person, but simultaneously, they are afraid of trying anything new or different and become extremely sensitive to the reactions and comments of anyone around.

The root cause of negative habit patterns can almost always be traced back to "destructive criticism" in early childhood. Often, destructive criticism is accompanied by physical punishment. In either or both cases, the child very quickly loses his or her natural spontaneity and becomes fearful and hypersensitive to others.

All the other fears that hold people back—the fears of loss, of poverty, of embarrassment, of ridicule, of ill health, of the loss of love, of public speaking, of taking a chance, of starting or trying something new or different—are rooted in the fears of failure and rejection that begin in early childhood.

THE ANTIDOTE TO ALL YOUR FEARS

One of the greatest discoveries in the development of the peak performance personality is that your fears and your level of self-esteem have an inverse or opposite relationship. In other words, the more you like yourself, the less you fear failure and rejection. The higher your levels of self-esteem, the lower are the fears and doubts that hold most people back. The more you like and value yourself, the more willing you are to take risks and to endure the inevitable setbacks, obstacles, and temporary failures that will occur. The more you like yourself, the less concerned you are with the approval or disapproval of other people. You go your own way.

The very fastest way to build your self-esteem and self-confidence, and to neutralize the fears that may be holding you back, is to repeat continually the words "I like myself!" Whenever you feel doubtful or uneasy, begin repeating these words to yourself, "I like myself! I like myself! I like myself!"

The most important million-dollar habit you can develop is the habit of deliberately building your own self-esteem and self-confidence on a daily basis. The more you feed your mind with positive words, pictures, and thoughts, the more positive, confident, optimistic, and unafraid you become. The more you like yourself, the better you do at anything you attempt. The more you like yourself, the less you fear failure and rejection. The more you like yourself, the less you worry about short-term setbacks and obstacles. The more you like yourself, the greater courage and resilience you will have to face the inevitable ups and downs of life. And the more you like yourself, the more you will persist until you succeed. Self-esteem is everything.

FULFILL YOUR COMPLETE POTENTIAL

There are four more mental laws you need to know and work with in order to fulfill your complete potential. The first of these is the Law of Habit. This law says, "Whatever you do repeatedly eventually becomes a new habit." In its simplest terms, this means you can develop any habit of thought or action you desire if you just repeat it often enough and long enough. We will talk about new habit formation and development in the next chapter.

The second law you must know and use is the Law of Emotion. This law says, "Every action that you take is stimulated by an emotion of some kind, either positive or negative."

You can think of emotions the way you would think of a campfire. In order for the campfire to continue burning, you must continue to put wood on the fire. If you stop putting fuel on the fire for any period of time, the fire will eventually go out.

The things you think about most of the time are very much like logs on the fire. If you think about what you want and how to get it most of the time, more and more of your mental abilities will be focused on achieving the goals you have set for yourself. But because your amount of "thinking time" is limited, when you discipline yourself to think only about what you want, you stop putting wood on the fire of your negative emotions. As a result, you begin to eliminate the doubts and fears that hold most people back.

Concentrate on What You Want

This brings us to the Law of Concentration. This law says, "Whatever you dwell upon, grows and expands in your life."

In other words, whatever you think about most of the time increases. More and more of your emotions and mental energies become focused and concentrated on what you are dwelling upon. The more you think about your goals and how to accomplish them, the faster you will move toward them. You will focus more of your emotional energy on them, and you will have less energy available for the problems, worries, and concerns that preoccupy most people.

The final law in this series is the Law of Subconscious activity. This law says, "Your subconscious mind accepts any thought, plan, or goal created by the conscious mind and then organizes your thoughts and behaviors to bring that goal into reality."

Whatever thoughts or goals you repeat over and over again in your conscious mind are eventually accepted by your subconscious mind. Your subconscious mind then goes to work, 24 hours a day, to coordinate your thoughts, words, and actions to bring those goals into your life.

One Thought at a Time

Your conscious mind can only hold one thought at a time, either positive or negative. You may be capable of thinking hundreds of thoughts in a row, but you can only think of one thought at a time. And you are always free to choose that thought. An essential success habit is the habit of keeping your mind focused clearly on the person you want to be, the goals you want to achieve, and the steps you must take to achieve those goals.

When you make a habit of thinking and talking most of the time about where you are going and how to get there, you take complete control of the development of your self-concept and your personality. You step on the accelerator of your own potential. You move yourself onto the fast track in your life. You begin to move ahead at a speed that will amaze you and everyone around you.

YOUR POTENTIAL IS UNLIMITED

You are a remarkable person, possessed of incredible untapped potentials and abilities. Whatever you have accomplished in life so far is only a shadow of what is truly possible for you. There are virtually no limits on what you can do, be, and have except for the limits you impose on yourself with your own thinking.

Of all creatures, only human beings can reprogram themselves and alter the courses of their lives. You can decide, right now, to take complete control of the shaping and sculpting of your self-concept and turn yourself into the very best person you can possibly imagine yourself becoming. By releasing your subconscious brakes—your fears of failure and rejection—and by building your self-esteem and self-confidence through positive self-talk, you can unlock your potential and accomplish any goal you can set for yourself.

By taking complete control of the development of your self-concept, you lay the foundation for the development of the million-dollar habits that will enable you to accomplish more in the next few years than the average person accomplishes in a lifetime.

Action Exercises

$ Identify the primary causes for the effects in your life. Why are you where you are, and what could you do differently to get different results?

$ On a scale of 1 to 10, how much do you feel that you are in control of your life? What could you do to increase your feelings of control?

$ What do you think about most of the time? What should you focus and concentrate on to improve your life?

Action Exercises, continued

$ What are the values, qualities, and attributes of other people that you most admire? What actions could you take to incorporate those values into your personality?

$ How much do you like yourself? What are the experiences that give you your greatest feelings of self-esteem, and how could you create more of them?

$ What are your greatest fears? How would you behave differently if you had no fears at all?

$ What can you do, starting today, to feed your mind with more of the thoughts, words, people, and pictures that are more consistent with the very best person you could be and the most important goals you want to achieve?

Man becomes a slave to his constantly repeated
acts. What he at first chooses, at last compels.

—ORISON SWETT MARDEN

3

Becoming a Person of Value

> Thoughts lead on to purposes; purposes go
> forth in action; actions form habits;
> habits decide character; and
> character fixes our destiny.
>
> —Tryon Edwards

*A*LMOST EVERYTHING YOU ARE OR WILL become will be determined by your thoughts, feelings, and behaviors. Most psychologists agree that fully 95 percent of everything you think, feel, and do will be determined by your habits. The key to becoming a great person, and living a great life, is for you to develop the habits of success that lead inevitably to your achieving everything that is possible for you.

Fortunately, all habits are learned and are therefore learnable. If you have bad habits or if you have not yet developed the habits that you need to help you reach your full potential, you can develop these good habits through a systematic process of practice and repetition.

Good habits are hard to learn but easy to live with. Bad habits, on the other hand, are easy to learn but hard to live with. In either case, once you have developed a habit, it becomes automatic and easy. Like breathing in and breathing out, you find it easier and easier to engage in thoughts, feelings, and behaviors that are consistent with the person you want to be and the goals you want to achieve.

WHERE HABITS ARE BORN

A habit has been defined as "a conditioned response to stimuli," but where do habits originate? A habit is developed as the result of your responding in a particular way to a particular stimulus, often starting early in life. It is very much like driving and following a fork in the road in one direction or another. Whichever direction you go, good or bad, largely determines where you end up.

Fortunately, you are born with no habits at all. You have acquired them all since infancy. Different habits take different time periods to develop if they are ones you desire or need to overcome, if they are ones you want to break. As it happens, there is a proven system that you can use to accelerate the process of new habit pattern development.

Behavioral psychologists refer to "operant conditioning" to describe how people learn certain automatic behaviors. They sometimes refer to the "SBC model" of new habit pattern formation. These three letters stand for "stimulus, behavior, and consequences." First, something happens in your life that stimulates a thought or feeling. Second, in response, you behave a particular way. Third, as a result, you experience a certain consequence. If you repeat this process often enough, you develop a new habit.

The Pavlovian Response

In experiments conducted by Russian scientist Ivan Pavlov with dogs—some of the first major experiments on the role of operant conditioning—a hungry dog was given a piece of meat while a bell was rung at the same time. This process was repeated several times, over several days. Each time the dog received the meat, the dog would salivate in anticipation of the food, and the bell would ring. After repeating this stimulus-response action several times, the dog would salivate automatically upon hearing the bell, even when no meat was present.

In the same way, you can develop conditioned responses to people and situations as the result of previous experiences, either positive or negative. For example, if there is someone in your life you love and care about, the thought of that person or the sound of that person on the phone will immediately cause you to smile and feel happy.

Conversely, if there is a person in your life, usually from your past, who has hurt you and made you angry or unhappy, the very thought of that person or even the person's name will immediately trigger feelings of anger or sadness. Many people become trapped by memories of unhappy experiences, which have become habitual responses, and are often unable to let them go.

As Simple as ABC

Another model of habit pattern development is called the "ABC Model." These three letters stand for "antecedents, behaviors, and consequences." What psychologists have discovered is that the antecedents, what has happened in the past, stimulate only 15 percent of your behaviors. Fully 85 percent of your behaviors are motivated by what you expect to happen in the future, by the anticipated consequences.

For example, if you are preparing to give a presentation or apply for a job, 85 percent of your motivation will be determined by what you expect to happen if you are successful. Only 15 percent of your motivation will be decided by what you have done in the past in similar circumstances.

Expectations Theory

A large block of work in psychology called "expectations theory" maintains that people are motivated to act in a particular way by what they expect to happen more than by any other factor or influence. In other words, you do the things you do because of the consequences you feel you will experience as a result. Expectations theory explains small things, like what you do and say in a social situation, and large matters, such as capital movements in the international financial markets.

As we discussed in Chapter 1, you can actually manufacture your own expectations. You can develop the habit of expecting good things to happen, no matter how they may appear at the moment. Your expectations then influence your attitudes and the way you treat other people. Your attitudes, expectations, and behaviors will then have an inordinate influence on the way things actually work out. In effect, you can control much of your own future by expecting things to happen in a positive way.

Unfortunately, negative expectations also become self-fulfilling prophecies. If you expect something to turn out poorly, this will affect your attitude and behavior. Your negative attitude then increases the likelihood that you will experience the negative consequences you anticipated. If you repeat this pattern often enough, you will develop a negative and pessimistic attitude. This way of thinking will become a habit.

NEW HABIT PATTERN DEVELOPMENT

How long does it take to develop a new habit? The time period can range from a single second to several years. The speed of new habit pattern development is largely determined by the intensity of the emotion that accompanies the decision to begin acting in a particular way.

Many people think, talk about, and resolve to lose weight and become physically fit. This may go on for years. Then one day, the doctor says, "If you don't get your weight down and improve your physical condition, you are in danger of dying at an early age."

Suddenly, the thought of dying can be so intense or frightening that the individual immediately changes diet, begins exercising, stops smoking, and becomes a healthy and fit person. Psychologists refer to this as a "significant emotional experience," or a "SEE." Any experience of intense joy or pain combined with a behavior can create a habitual behavior pattern that may endure for the rest of a person's life.

For example, putting your hand on a hot stove or touching a live electrical wire will give you an intense and immediate pain or shock. The experience may only take a split second. But for the rest of your life, you will possess the habit of not putting your hand on hot stoves or touching live electrical wires. The habit will have been formed instantly and endure permanently.

According to the experts, it takes about 21 days to form a habit pattern of medium complexity. By this, we mean simple habits such as getting up earlier, exercising each morning before you start out, listening to audio programs in your car, going to bed at a certain hour, being punctual for appointments, planning every day in advance, starting with your most important tasks each day, or completing your tasks before you start something else. These are habits of medium complexity that can be quite easily developed in 14 to 21 days through practice and repetition.

How do you develop a new habit? Over the years, a simple, powerful, proven methodology has been determined for new habit development. It is very much like a recipe for preparing a dish in the kitchen. You can use it to develop any habit that you desire. Over time, you will find it easier and easier to develop the habits that you want to incorporate into your personality.

SEVEN STEPS TO A NEW HABIT

1. MAKE A DECISION.

Decide clearly that you are going to begin acting in a specific way 100 percent of the time. For example, if you decide to rise early and exercise each morning, set your clock for a specific time; when the alarm goes off, immediately get up, put on your exercise clothes, and begin your exercise session.

2. NEVER ALLOW AN EXCEPTION.

Do not make exceptions to your new habit pattern during the formative stages. Don't make excuses or rationalizations. Don't let yourself off the hook. If you resolve to get up at 6:00 A.M. each morning, discipline yourself to get up at 6:00 A.M., every single morning until this becomes automatic.

3. TELL OTHERS.

Inform people around you that you are going to begin practicing a partic-ular behavior. It is amazing how much more disciplined and determined you will become when you know others are watching you to see if you have the willpower to follow through on your resolution.

4. VISUALIZE YOURSELF.

In your mind's eye, see yourself performing or behaving in a particular way in a particular situation. The more often you visualize and imagine yourself acting as if you already had the new habit, the more rapidly this new behavior will be accepted by your subconscious mind and become automatic.

5. CREATE AN AFFIRMATION.

Repeat the affirmation over and over to yourself. This repetition dramati-cally increases the speed at which you develop the new habit. For example, you can say something like, "I get up and get going immediately at 6:00 each morning!" Repeat these words the last thing before you fall asleep. In most cases, you will automatically wake up minutes before the alarm clock goes off, and soon you will need no alarm clock at all.

6. RESOLVE TO PERSIST.

Keep practicing the new behavior until it is so automatic and easy that you actually feel uncomfortable when you do not do what you have decided to do.

7. REWARD YOURSELF.

Most important, give yourself a treat of some kind for practicing the new behavior. Each time you reward yourself, you reaffirm and rein-force the behavior. Soon you begin to associate, at an unconscious level, the pleasure of the reward with the behavior. You set up your own force

Overcoming Procrastination

Procrastination is a problem that bothers almost everyone. Learning to overcome it is an exercise that will pay off for you all your life. To overcome procrastination, you can practice the seven steps described above.

First, make a decision to start immediately on your most important task each day. Second, never allow an exception until the habit is firmly entrenched. Third, tell others that you are going to stop procrastinating in a particular area. Fourth, visualize and imagine yourself starting right in on a task and working at it nonstop until it is complete. Fifth, repeat over and over, "I start and work immediately on my most important task." Sixth, discipline yourself to persist every day until it becomes automatic for you to start immediately on your top task. And seventh, reward yourself each time you overcome procrastination and complete an important job. Ever after, practice this process on any new habit you want to develop.

Make developing new habits a regular part of your life. Always be working on developing a new habit that can help you. One new habit per month will amount to 12 new habits each year, 60 new, life-enhancing habits every five years. At that rate, your life would change so profoundly that you would become a whole new person in a very positive way.

---

field of positive consequences that you unconsciously look forward to as the result of engaging in the behavior or habit that you have decided upon.

TAKE IT EASY ON YOURSELF

Where do you start in new habit pattern development? When people first learn about the importance of developing new habits and how positive patterns of thought and behavior can have a wonderful effect on their lives, they often make the mistake of resolving to develop several new habits at once. They decide to improve in every area of their lives simultaneously.

Permanent Fixtures of Your Mind

As it happens, old habits do not die. They don't disappear. When you stop practicing them and discipline yourself instead to behave in a new way, the old habits become weak and withdraw into your subconscious mind. Your new habits may override and replace the old habits, but you never eliminate them completely. They lurk below the surface, waiting to reemerge at a later time, when the stimulus that originally created them is repeated.

For example, when you were young, you learned how to ride a bicycle. Eventually, you began driving a car. Many years, even decades later, you can get onto a bicycle and within a few seconds, you can be riding with the same balance and skill that you had programmed into your subconscious mind as a child.

Many people first learned how to drive a car with a standard transmission, a stick shift. Today, most cars have automatic transmissions. You may drive one for years. However, if you were required to drive a car with a stick shift, even after many years, you would slip into the old habit of shifting gears easily and naturally in a few seconds. The old habits never completely go away.

They very excitedly draw up a list of new habits that they desire for their work, their financial lives, their business activities, their relationships, their family, their health, and their personal organization skills. As a result, they very quickly hit a mental wall, and no improvement takes place at all.

Here is the rule in developing new habits: be patient with yourself. It has taken you an entire lifetime to become the person you are. It is not possible for you to change everything overnight. You should therefore select a single habit that you feel can be more helpful to you at the moment than any other particular habit. Write it down and create a positive affirmation, combined with a visual image, of yourself acting exactly as if you already had that new habit.

You then launch immediately and never allow an exception. Talk to yourself positively and tell yourself that you already have this habit.

Imagine yourself behaving as though you had already learned this behavior. Tell others. Give yourself rewards and reinforcement each time you engage in the new behavior. But only try to change one habit at a time.

BEING AND BECOMING

You are unique in the entire world. There never has been, nor will there ever be, anyone just like you. And what makes you different and special is your mind. It is your ability to think, to decide, and to act.

The sum total of your thinking and experiences in your past is contained in your actions of today, in your habitual ways of reacting and responding to other people. It is only your actions that tell who you are and what you have become.

The good news is that you are not just a human being. You are a "human becomingness." You are in a continual state of growth and evolution, shedding old ideas and habits and developing new ones. It doesn't matter where you are coming from; all that really matters is where you are going. And where you are going is only limited by your own imagination.

Action Exercises

$ What one habit would you like to have, more than anything else? What one action could you take immediately to begin developing this habit?

$ What are the most important results or consequences that you want to enjoy? What habits would help you the most to achieve them?

$ Select one habit you would like to develop in your financial life and activities; define it clearly and then begin work on it today.

$ Select one habit you would like to develop in your family life and the way you interact with others; begin practicing it today.

Action Exercises, continued

$ Select one health habit that could contribute to your health and fitness more that anything else you could do; start it today.

$ Select one habit that would help you to be more effective and productive at work, and begin acting as if you already had that habit.

$ Imagine that you have no limitations on what you could do, have, or be, or on the habits you could develop. What goals would you set for yourself?

What happens to a man is less significant
than what happens within him."

—Louis L. Mann

4

The Habits You Need to Succeed

> Self command is not only itself a great
> virtue, but from it all the other virtues
> seem to derive their principle luster.
>
> —ADAM SMITH

*T*HE MOST IMPORTANT HABIT YOU CAN develop for success, achievement, and happiness is the habit of self-discipline. Perhaps the best definition of self-discipline comes from author and publisher Elbert Hubbard, "Self-discipline is the ability to make yourself do what you should do, when you should do it, whether you feel like it or not."

The habit of self-discipline is closely tied to the Law of Control that we talked about earlier. As you recall, the Law of Control says, "You feel happy about yourself to the degree to which you feel you are in control of your own life."

Self-discipline is the key to self-mastery and self-control. The more capable you become of disciplining yourself to do what you have decided to do, whether you feel like it or not, the more positive and powerful you will feel.

THE SOURCE OF PERSONAL POWER

There is a direct relationship between self-discipline and self-esteem. The more you discipline yourself to behave in the manner that you have decided, the more you will like and respect yourself. You will feel more positive and confident, and you will become stronger and more in charge of your life and situation.

Every act of self-discipline strengthens every other discipline at the same time. Every weakness in self-discipline weakens your other disciplines as well. Like working a muscle, your ability to discipline yourself to behave in the way that you have decided grows stronger each time you exercise it. This is why the happiest, most successful, and most respected men and women in our society are all men and women of great self-control, self-mastery and self-discipline. And this is a habit you can learn, with practice.

BECOME A LIFELONG OPTIMIST

Perhaps the most helpful mental habit you can develop is the habit of optimism. Optimists are usually the happiest, healthiest, most successful, and most influential people in every group and society. According to Dr. Martin Seligman, professor of psychology at the University of Pennsylvania, in his book *Learned Optimism* (Knopf, 1991), people learn to become optimists by thinking the way optimists think. They in effect learn to be optimists just as pessimists learn to be pessimistic.

We said earlier that the greatest discovery and the summary statement of much of psychology, religion, and philosophy, is, "You become what you think about most of the time."

What is it that optimists think about most of the time? In its simplest terms, optimists think about what they want and how to get it, most of the time. They think about where they are going and how to get there. The very idea of thinking about what they want makes them happy and positive. It increases their energy and releases their creativity. It motivates and stimulates them to perform at higher levels.

Pessimists, on the other hand, are the opposite. They think and talk about what they don't want most of the time. They think about the people they don't like, the problems that they are having, or have had in the past, and especially, they think about who is to blame for their particular situation. And the more they think about the things they don't want and who to blame for their problems, the more negative and angry they become. The more negative they become, the faster they attract into their lives exactly those things that they do not want to happen.

Develop a Hardy Personality

A relatively new field of medicine called "psychoneuroimmunology" is developing. Research in this area has concluded that the quality of your thinking has an enormous impact on the strength of your immune system. The habit of optimism, combined with a positive mental attitude, seems to strengthen and increase the body's t-cells, which are responsible for resisting and overcoming the various factors that contribute to disease and illnesses of all kinds.

Psychologists have now developed a profile of what they call the "hardy personality." This is the man or woman who seems to respond positively and effectively to adversity and setbacks. He or she is optimistic and forward thinking. It seems that the more optimistic you are, the stronger and more resilient your mind and body. As a result, you will have higher levels of energy and a quicker recovery rate from fatigue. You will seldom be ill for any reason. If you catch a cold or flu, which will be rare, you will bounce back quickly as the fortified t-cells in your body quickly counterattack and eradicate the infection that is causing it.

Think about What You Want

You develop the habit of optimism by disciplining yourself to keep your thoughts and words on what you want and off of what you don't want. You become an optimist by thinking continually in terms of the specific actions you can take immediately to achieve the goals that are most important to you. The busier you become working toward the accomplishment of goals and objectives that you have set for yourself, the more energy and enthusiasm you will have, the faster you will move ahead, the more you will get done, and the happier you will be.

Radio personality Earl Nightingale once wrote, "Happiness is the progressive realization of a worthy ideal." When you are working hour by hour and day by day toward the achievement of something that is worthwhile and important to you, your brain releases a steady stream of endorphins that gives you a feeling of happiness and well-being. You feel more positive and creative. You have more energy and enthusiasm. This positive feeling acts as a reward or reinforcement that motivates you continually to think the thoughts and take the actions that move you even more rapidly in the direction of your hopes, dreams, and goals.

THE ORIENTATIONS OF HIGH PERFORMANCE

Optimistic people think very differently than pessimistic people. They develop a series of "orientations" or general tendencies of thinking that separate them from the average person. These orientations soon become habitual ways of thinking and acting that propel them forward toward the success and happiness they desire. Like all habits, these ways of thinking are learnable through practice and repetition.

As you develop the habits of thinking in these ways most of the time, you become a different person. In a way, these are the habits of "mental fitness." Just as you would become physically fit if you went to a health club and worked out with the equipment regularly, you become mentally fit, positive, and optimistic as you work out your mind practicing these orientations.

Think about the Future

The first way of thinking practiced by optimists is *future orientation.* Optimists are those who develop the habit of "idealization." In the process of idealizing, you take your thoughts off the present situation and instead imagine a perfect future for yourself in your business, your finances, your family, your health, or any other area. You imagine that you have a "magic wand" that you could wave and create your ideal future vision. Instead of worrying or becoming preoccupied with the details of the present moment, you ask yourself, "What would I ideally like to be, have, or do sometime in the future?"

You develop the habit of practicing "back from the future" thinking. In this type of thinking, you project forward into the future to your ideal result and imagine what it would look like in every way. You then look back to the present and ask yourself, "What would I have to do, starting today, to create the ideal future that I desire?"

You develop the habit of "long-time perspective." Instead of focusing continually on the moment and on immediate actions and gratification, you think long-term about what you want and where you are going. The greater clarity you have with regard to the results you want to achieve in the future, the better and more accurate will be your decisions in the present moment. When you idealize and practice long-term thinking, you find yourself setting much better goals and priorities in your day-to-day life.

Think about Your Goals

Goal orientation is the second quality or way of thinking practiced by optimists and all successful people. In future orientation, you develop a clear, ideal image of what you want to accomplish sometime in the future. With goal orientation, you crystallize that image into specific, measurable, detailed goals and objectives you will need to accomplish to achieve that ideal future vision.

Successful people soon develop the habits of personal strategic planning. They sit down and make a list of exactly what they want to accomplish in the short-, medium-, and long-term. They then use a powerful, seven-part goal-setting methodology to create blueprints and plans of action that they follow every day.

Once you develop the habit of setting goals and making plans for their accomplishment, it will become as natural for you as breathing. By following a proven goal setting process, you will increase the likelihood of achieving your goals by as much as ten times, by 1,000 percent or more. This is just not a theory; it has been proven and demonstrated on a national basis.

In February 2003, *USA Today* reported on a study of people who had set New Year's resolutions the year before. They found that only 4 percent of the people who had made New Year's resolutions, but had not put them in writing, followed through on them. But 46 percent of those people who had written down their New Year's resolutions carried them out. This is a difference in success rates of more than 1,100 percent!

THE SEVEN STEP FORMULA FOR GOAL SETTING

Many formulas and recipes exist for goal setting. As a rule, "any plan is better than no plan at all." Here is one of the best and most effective goal-setting plans or formulas you will ever learn.

STEP ONE
Decide exactly what you want in a specific area and write it down clearly, in detail. Make it measurable and specific.

STEP TWO
Set a deadline for the achievement of the goal. If it is a large goal, break it down into smaller parts and set sub-deadlines.

STEP THREE
Make a list of everything that you will have to do to achieve this goal. As you think of new items, add them to your list until it is complete.

STEP FOUR
Organize your list of action steps into a plan. A plan is organized on the basis of two elements, priority and sequence.

In organizing by priorities, you determine the most important things that you can possibly do on your list to achieve your goal. The 80/20 Rule applies: 20 percent of the things that you do will account for 80 percent of your results. If you do not set clear priorities, you will "major in minors" and spend much of your time doing small and irrelevant tasks that do not help you to achieve the goal.

In organizing by sequence, you determine what has to be done before something else can be done. There are always activities that are dependent upon other activities being completed in advance. What are they, and what is the logical order or sequence?

STEP FIVE

Identify the obstacles or limitations that might hold you back from achieving your goal, both in the situation and within yourself. Ask yourself, "Why have I not achieved this goal already?"

Identify the most important constraint or limitation that is holding you back, and then focus on removing that obstacle. It could be a certain amount of money or a key resource. It could be an additional skill or habit that you need. It could be additional information you require. It could be the help or assistance of one or more people. Whatever it is, identify it clearly and go to work to eliminate it.

STEP SIX

Once you have determined your goal, developed your plan, and identified your major obstacle, immediately take action of some kind toward the achievement of your goal. Step out in faith. Do the first thing that comes to mind. But do something immediately to start the process of goal attainment moving forward.

STEP SEVEN

Do something every day that moves you toward your most important goal. Make a habit of getting up each morning, planning your day, and then doing something, anything, that moves you at least one step closer to what is most important to you.

The habit of doing something every single day that moves you toward an important goal develops within you the power of momentum. Daily action deepens your belief that the goal is achievable and activates the Law of Attraction. As a result, you begin moving faster and faster toward your goal, and your goal begins moving faster and faster toward you.

I have spoken to people all over the world, for many years, who have told me that the habit of taking action every day on one or more of their major goals has been life-transforming. They have told me that this single habit has been more responsible for their success than any other idea they ever learned. Try it for yourself and see.

SET YOUR GOALS EACH DAY

One of the most important habits you can develop is the habit of daily goal setting. Countless people I have taught this to have told me over the years that the power of this process is absolutely incredible!

Daily goal setting is quite simple. Get a spiral notebook to write your goals in and resolve to keep it nearby for the rest of your life. Each morning, before you start out, open your spiral notebook and start a new page. I always begin with the words "My goals are the following: . . ."

You then write down your top 10 to 15 goals in the present tense, as though you have already achieved them. Your subconscious mind is only activated by commands that are stated in the present, positive, personal tense. So instead of writing a goal such as, "I am going to lose weight in the months ahead," you would write instead, "I weigh xxx number of pounds by (a specific date.)"

Instead of saying, "I will earn more money over the next year," you would say, "I earn X number of dollars by such and such a date."

The more specific you can be in terms of what you want and when you want to achieve it, expressed in the positive, present tense, and beginning with the word "I," the more powerful the effect will be on your subconscious mind. Goals written and stated in this way activate the Laws of Expectations and Attraction. They cause you to develop new beliefs about what is possible for you. They activate the Laws of Emotion and Correspondence. They increase your energy and stimulate your creativity.

Positive, personal, present-tense goals, written down repeatedly each day activate your subconscious and superconscious minds and step on the accelerator of your own potential. As a result, you start to move more rapidly toward the achievement of your goals, and they begin to move more rapidly toward you.

THINK ABOUT EXCELLENT PERFORMANCE

An important habit of thinking developed by optimists is the habit of *excellence orientation*. The fact is that, to achieve something you have never achieved before, you will have to develop and master one or more skills that you have never had before. By the Law of Correspondence, your outer world will always be a reflection of your inner world. If you want to change something in your outer world or achieve a goal that you've never achieved in the past, you are going to have to change your inner world in some way. Almost invariably, this requires the acquisition of a new skill or set of skills.

Here is the good news. A skill is the same as a habit of performance, and like habits, all skills are learnable. You can learn any skill you need to learn to achieve any goal that you can set for yourself. If anyone else around you has developed a key skill that has enabled him or her to be more successful, that is proof in itself that you too can learn and develop this skill. It is simply a matter of practice and repetition.

IDENTIFY YOUR KEY SKILLS

Excellence orientation requires that you make a list of the key skills that are essential for success in your field. Usually, only about five to seven skills, or key result areas, determine most of the success in any field of endeavor. Your first job is to identify these key skills and write them down.

Here is an interesting discovery. You have achieved your level of success in your field today because of your talent and ability in certain key areas. But at the same time, you are being held back by your weaknesses in other areas. The rule is that your weakest key skill determines the height of your results and your income. In other words, you could be excellent at six out of seven key result areas, but your weakness in the seventh area will determine your overall results and rewards in that job or field.

You therefore ask yourself this question, "What one skill, if I developed and did it consistently in an excellent fashion, would have the greatest positive impact on my career?"

This is one of the most important questions that you ask and answer throughout your career. You must develop the habit of continually identifying and working on your weakest key skill. Bringing up your ability in this one area will usually have a greater and more immediate impact on your results than anything else you can do.

If you do not know the answer to this question (and most people don't), go to your boss or your co-workers and ask them, "What one skill, if I developed and did it in an excellent fashion, would help me the most in my job?"

Pick Up the Pace

Sometimes I ask my audiences, "If a group of children goes for a walk, which child determines the speed of the entire group?" They will always reply and say, "The slowest child." Exactly.

Your "slowest kid" is your weakest key skill. It sets the speed at which you move ahead in your career and determines the heights that you reach. And here is another important point. You are almost invariably weak in an area that you do not particularly like or enjoy. But the reason that you do not like or enjoy that area is because you have not yet mastered that area. As soon as you write it down, make a plan, and develop excellence in a particular skill area, you will like and enjoy performing in that area for the rest of your career.

The fact is you could be only one skill away from doubling your productivity, your performance, and your income. The acquisition of one key skill where you are currently weak could make it possible for you to use all your other skills at a higher level and accomplish more in your work than you ever thought possible. What one skill could that be?

Decide today to develop the habit of excellence orientation. Resolve to join the top 10 percent of performers in your field. Find out what you have to do, and how much you have to earn to be in the top 10 percent. Set it as a goal. Make a plan and work on your plan to develop the essential skills you need every single day. In no time at all, you will be amazed at how quickly your life changes for the better.

The Pursuit of Mastery

The reason many people underachieve in their careers is because they do not realize how long it takes to achieve mastery in any field. Extensive research in this area suggests that it requires about five to seven years of hard work for you to move to the top of your field. This means five to seven years of focused, concentrated, determined work on yourself to get better and better in the key result areas responsible for your results and rewards. And there are no short cuts.

Sometimes people say to me, "Five to seven years is a long time to achieve mastery in my field." This is true. But I then remind that, "The time is going to pass anyway."

This is very important. The biggest regret many people report is "not starting early enough." But the time is going to pass anyway. Five to seven years from now, five to seven years will have passed. The only question is, "Where are you going to be five to seven years from now in your field?"

The good news is, if you set it as a goal, make a plan, and work on it every day, five to seven years from now you are going to be in the top 10 percent of people in your field. You are going to be one of the highest paid and most respected people in your career. You are going to be enjoying the great results and rewards of the top performers in your business.

Remember this: Nobody is better than you, and nobody is smarter than you. If someone is doing better than you, it just means they started work on themselves in a certain way earlier than you did. And whatever anyone else has done, you can do as well. There are no limits except the limits you place on yourself with your own thinking.

The very fact that others have been able to excel in a field, after having started off in that field with no experience or skills, is proof that you can excel in that field as well. Your job is to put your head down, get busy, and go to work on yourself. Resolve today to develop the habit of personal

Increase Your Income 1,000 Percent?

In my book *Focal Point* (Anacom, 2002), I explain my 1,000 percent formula in detail. In summary, it says: if you work on yourself continually, you can increase your productivity, performance, and output by 1/10th of 1 percent (1/1,000th) each working day.

1/10th of 1 percent per day improvement translates into approximately 1/2 of 1 percent per week.

1/2 of 1 percent per week improvement translates into 2 percent improvement per month.

2 percent improvement per month translates into about 26 percent improvement in productivity, performance, and output each year.

Almost anyone who dedicates himself to continuous personal growth and learning can upgrade his performance and productivity by 26 percent each year. An improvement of 26 percent each year, compounded year by year, means you will double your productivity, performance, and output in 2.7 years.

Over the course of ten years, by improving yourself by 1/1,000th per day (1/10th of one percent), 26 percent per year, you will increase your productivity, performance, and rewards by 1,004 percent. This is an increase in your income of ten times!

Not long ago, I was giving a daylong seminar in Seattle. A young man approached me at the break and reminded me he had been through my program and had learned this 1,000 percent formula some years ago, when he was in his early 20s.

He said, "I just wanted to tell you personally that your formula doesn't work."

As you can imagine, I was a bit surprised. I asked him, "How do you mean?"

He smiled broadly and said, "It's too conservative. It doesn't take ten years. It only took me seven years to increase my income ten times by following that formula every single day. Last year, I earned exactly ten times what I was earning when I first heard that formula from you when I was 23 years old."

He told me that his income as a car salesman seven years ago had been $35,000 per year. In the previous year, he had earned more than $350,000 and is now one of the top marketing consultants in the automobile industry in the Pacific Northwest. His previous employer pays him as much today, on retainer as a consultant, as he used to pay him for working full time.

Are these kind of results possible for you? Of course they are! The Law of Cause and Effect says that if you do what other successful people do, you will eventually get the same results other successful people get. This is not a wish or theory; it is a universal law. The law itself is neutral. It works for everybody, everywhere.

---

excellence and focus all your energies on joining the top 10 percent of professionals in your field. Once you do that, your entire future will open up in front of you. You will become unstoppable.

COMMIT TO LIFELONG LEARNING

Another key habit of thinking and acting practiced by top people is *growth orientation*. It is the high road to excellent performance and essential to developing the habit of optimism. This method of thinking and living is the foundation of excellence orientation and is essential for you to develop if you want to move into the top 10 percent of your field.

Growth orientation requires that you develop the habit of continuous learning, the habit of continuous personal and professional development. Just as you exercise physically on a regular basis to remain fit and healthy, you must exercise mentally on a daily basis to become better and better in your chosen field.

Three Steps onto the Fast Track

There are three parts of the continuous learning process. By practicing these activities daily, weekly, and monthly, you will increase your productivity, performance, and output by 1/10th of 1 percent per day, compounded. You will eventually become one of the highest paid and most successful people in your field. There are no exceptions.

READ EVERY DAY

Arise early each morning and read for 30 to 60 minutes in your field. Underline and take notes. Think of how you can apply what you are learning to your day-to-day work. Throughout the day, think of how you can use what you read to be more effective. At the end of each day, review the day based on your new knowledge and skills and evaluate your results and progress.

There is an important psychological principle called the "Hawthorne effect." In short, what this principle says is, "The very act of paying attention to a particular behavior causes you to improve your performance in that area."

For example, if you decided that you were going to develop the habit of listening more closely to people when they speak and interrupting less, the very act of thinking about listening would cause you to become a better listener.

If you decided that you were going to focus on punctuality each day until you developed punctuality as a habit, the very act of thinking about being more punctual would cause you to become more punctual in your personal and professional life. The more you think about a behavior, the better you will become in that area.

When you read in your field for 30 to 60 minutes each day and think throughout the day about how you could apply what you have learned, you will tend to become better and better at what you do, both consciously and unconsciously. The improved results you get will accumulate and compound over time. You will become better and better at what you do almost without being aware of it.

If you read 30 to 60 minutes each day, you should complete about one book per week. The average American reads less than one book per year. If you read one book per week, you should finish at least 50 books each year. As it happens, earning a Ph.D. from a major university requires the reading and synthesis into a dissertation of about 40 to 50 books.

If you were to read one book per week, 50 books per year, you would be getting the equivalent of a practical Ph.D. in your field each year. If you continued reading at this level, 50 books per year, you would read 500 books in the next ten years. If you were to read 500 books in your field, in a world where the average person reads less than one book per year, do you think you might gain an edge?

The fact is, you would become one of the best-read, most knowledgeable, most expert, and highest-paid practioners in your field if you were simply to develop the habit of reading in your field each morning for 30 to 60 minutes. I have never met anyone, anywhere, throughout the world, who has not transformed their lives and their careers by the habit of daily reading.

You must discipline yourself to leave the television or radio off, to put the newspaper aside, perhaps to rise a little earlier in the morning, so you can invest in your mind. This investment will give you one of the highest payoffs in terms of results, rewards, and satisfaction that you will ever enjoy from anything you do.

LEARN FROM THE EXPERTS

The second habit you need for continuous learning is the habit of attending every seminar and course you possibly can. Do not make the mistake of waiting for courses and seminars to come to you or waiting for your company to organize and pay for additional training. You are completely responsible for your own life, which includes your own personal and professional development. No one cares as much about your future and your career as you do. No one cares about your ability to increase your income and move into the top 10 percent of your field as much as you do. You are responsible.

Over the years, I have spoken to more than two million men and women in 25 countries. I have filing cabinets full of letters, faxes, and e-mails from my students and seminar participants. Many of them write and tell me that they will travel across the country in order to attend a seminar or workshop given by an expert or specialist in their field. They will invest enormous amounts of time and money to acquire the additional specialized skills they need to move ahead more rapidly in their field.

Over and over, my students tell me that they have sometimes saved themselves years of hard work as the result of attending a single program. Some of them have even gone to the top of their fields and become millionaires as the result of learning one new set of skills that was relevant and immediately applicable to their field.

There is something remarkable that takes place in an adult learning situation. It is very different from attending a required course in college or university. The type of people who attend adult seminars are a much higher caliber than you meet in your day-to-day life. They are more positive, more highly motivated, have bigger and better goals, and are more determined to succeed. When you spend several hours in their company, it has a subtle but powerful subconscious effect on you. You actually become a better and more focused person by the very act of associating with other successful people in an adult learning situation or seminar.

Make it a habit to seek out and attend at least four seminar programs per year in your field. If your organization has annual or national conventions, be sure to attend. Eagerly seek out and sit in on the most important talks and lectures at each of these workshops or annual meetings. Sometimes, one good idea from an expert in your field can transform your entire career.

ATTEND UNIVERSITY ON WHEELS

The third habit you need for continuous learning is the habit of listening to audio programs in your car and as you walk or exercise. Audio learning is considered by many to be the greatest breakthrough in education since the invention of the printing press. And I agree.

I discovered audio learning at the age of 23. I was frustrated, working long hours, and broke. When I began to listen to audio programs on a portable cassette player that I carried with me, my life was transformed in a way I never thought possible. By learning the critical skills of selling from experienced professionals who had been selling my product for many years, I was able to go from the bottom of my sales force to the top in less than six months.

Eventually, I became a sales manager and trained dozens of people in the same techniques. Over the years, I have trained hundreds of thousands of sales professionals in the very best skills and methodologies ever discovered in professional selling. Many of them have gone onto become sales leaders and even millionaires as a result. My own audio program, *The Psychology of Selling* has become the top-selling program of its kind in the world, produced in 16 languages.

The average person spends 500 to 1,000 hours each year in his or her car. This is the equivalent of three to six months of 40-hour weeks, or the equivalent of one or two university semesters.

In fact, the University of Southern California recently concluded that a person could get the equivalent of almost full-time university attendance simply by listening to educational audio programs as she drove from place to place during the course of the week.

Reid Buckley, a professional speaker, once said, "If you are not continually learning and upgrading your skills, somewhere, someone else is. And when you meet that person, you will lose."

The Race Is On

There is a race on today, and you are in it, whether you know it or not. If you have not yet developed the habit of reading each day, attending seminars and courses regularly, and listening to audio programs in your car as you move around, somewhere, someone else is taking those steps. Inevitably, that person will win the race, and you will lose.

The good news is that an average person who develops the habit of lifelong learning will eventually run circles around a genius who goes home and watches television each night. There is perhaps no habit that will more guarantee your success in life than the habit of continuous personal and professional improvement.

The payoff in improved results in your field will be tremendous. But the best payoff of all is that you will become more positive and optimistic. You will have more energy, be more creative, and be a happier person as you continue to grow and grow toward the realization of your full potential.

The habit of continuous learning enables average people to become top performers in their fields. It enables people to go from rags to riches.

It enables people to rise from poverty and frustration to affluence and success. Continuous learning opens every door for you. It increases your intelligence and creativity and puts you onto the fast track in your career. Continuous learning, like nature, is neutral. Anyone can use it to accomplish extraordinary things in life. It is one of the best habits you can ever develop, and the payoff from continuous learning will last you all the days of your life.

YOU DETERMINE YOUR OWN DESTINY

Each person is essentially self-made. The person you are may have been determined by your childhood experiences. But the person that you become, the person that you may be, is completely under your own control. The great principle "you become what you think about most of the time" refers to what you are thinking today, at this very moment. It is not your thinking of the past, or your thinking in the future, that determines the course of your destiny. Everything you are, and everything you will be, is determined by the thoughts that you think at each moment. And you can take complete control of those thoughts at any time you decide to.

You become an optimist by taking control of your inner dialogue, your self-talk. Resolve today to develop the habit of talking to yourself in a positive way. Say things to yourself such as, "I like myself!" Say, "I can do it!" over and over again. If someone asks you how you are feeling today, always reply by saying "I feel terrific!" When you think about your job, repeat to yourself, "I love my work! I love my work!"

Most psychologists feel that fully 95 percent of your emotions are determined by the things you think and the words you say to yourself as you go through your day. Use your self-discipline and self-control to think and talk about the things you want, rather than allowing your mind to become preoccupied with the things that you don't want or that you doubt and fear.

What You See Is What You Will Be

The most powerful affirmation or message you can send from your conscious mind to your subconscious mind is a visualization or mental image. Develop the habit of creating clear, positive, exciting pictures of yourself performing at your best and visions of your goals as if they were already achieved.

Each time you create a mental image in your conscious mind, you send a message that activates your subconscious mind, triggers the Law of Attraction, stimulates your creativity, and moves you toward the realization of that mental picture in your external world.

Positive, successful people make a habit of continually visualizing the outcomes that they desire, thereby programming their subconscious minds and shaping their self-image and their external performance.

Best of all is when you combine positive self-talk with positive mental imaging. You talk about the things you want, and you create exciting mental pictures of your goals and desires as if they already existed in your reality. Positive thoughts and words make you more optimistic, give you more energy, enable you to bounce back faster from disappointment, and keep you moving forward throughout the day.

Feed Your Mind with Mental Protein

Develop the habit of feeding your mind with positive mental food. Remember, you are very susceptible to the suggested influences in your environment, whether they are radio, television, newspapers, magazines, billboards, or conversations with other people. Your mind is your most important and precious asset. You must protect it and keep it clean, clear, and focused on what you want, rather than allowing it to be polluted by the negative influences around you.

Refuse to watch terror or trash on television. Refuse to read about all the murders, robberies, rapes, and tragedies in the newspapers. Refuse to listen to endless hours of mindless radio commentary on all the problems in the modern world. Refuse to engage in endless conversations with people about all the political and social problems in your nation or community. Keep your mind clean, clear, positive, and free.

Not only do you become what you think about, but you also become what you feed into your mind on a regular basis. If you want to be positive, optimistic, and happy, continually feed your mind with positive books and articles, positive audio learning programs, positive input and information from other experts in your field, and positive conversations with other optimistic, goal-oriented people who are going somewhere with their lives.

Get around the Right People

Make it a habit to associate only with the kind of people that you like, admire, respect, and want to be like. Do not drink coffee with the person who happens to be sitting in the breakroom. Do not go out for lunch with the person who happens to be near the door. Do not socialize after work with anyone who invites you. Be very conscientious and clear about the kind of people you are going to allow to influence your thinking and feelings with their conversations and opinions.

Dr. David McClelland of Harvard found that your "reference group" would determine as much as 95 percent of your success or failure in life. Your reference group is the people you habitually associate with and consider yourself to be one of. These can be members of your family; your co-workers; or members of your political party, church, or social organizations. The fact is, "Birds of a feather flock together." Or as motivational speaker Zig Ziglar says, "You can't fly with the eagles if you continue to scratch with the turkeys."

TAKE ACTION ON YOUR GOALS AND PLANS

Finally, in becoming everything that you are capable of becoming, develop the habit of action orientation. In every study of successful people, in virtually every field, the quality of action orientation emerges as the most outwardly identifiable quality of people who are going somewhere in their lives and careers.

Action orientation means that you develop the habit of moving quickly when you have an idea or opportunity. You think continually in terms of the specific actions you can take to move closer to achieving a goal or getting a result that is important to you. Instead of talking endlessly about what you are going to do in the future, you act immediately to do something in the present.

Winners and Losers

The American Management Association reported on a study of managers who had been divided into two groups, those whose careers has flattened and those whose careers were moving upward and onward at a rapid rate. They interviewed both groups to try to determine the differences that accounted for their relative levels of success and failure.

What they finally concluded was that the difference could not be accounted for by education, experience, background, networking, or intelligence. The critical difference between success and failure was contained in the habit of taking the initiative. Managers and executives who were on the fast track were constantly moving out of their comfort zone and taking the initiative to try new things in new areas.

On the other hand, managers who were being continually passed over for promotion were continually waiting for someone to come along and tell them what to do. Once they had been given clear instructions, they seemed to be quite competent at carrying out their responsibilities. But the idea of initiating in the first place was alien to them.

You Can Do It

Once you have defined your ideal future, set and determine your goals and plans, developed a strategy for achieving excellence in your field, and committed yourself to continuous learning, develop the habit of moving quickly and taking the initiative in each area of your life that is important to you. Instead of waiting for things to happen, develop the habit of making things happen. Instead of waiting for things to get better, take the initiative to change or improve whatever situation you find yourself in.

It is not easy to change your entire way of thinking and become an extraordinary person as the result of your own efforts and your own work on yourself. But it is definitely possible, when you accept complete responsibility and take full control over the evolution and development of your own character and personality.

The most important part of this chapter, and this book, is action. It is not what you read or learn but the specific actions that you take.

Researchers have found that there is a direct relationship between how quickly you take action on a new idea and how likely it is that you will ever take action on any idea at all. The very act of moving quickly in one area seems to develop the habit of moving quickly in other areas.

If you have learned something that is important to you in this chapter or if you have an idea about something that you can do immediately to improve some part of your life, resolve to take action on it immediately. Do it now. Develop a sense of urgency. Hurry. Resolve to become known as the kind of person who moves fast on any new idea or possibility. This can be one of the most important habits you ever develop.

Action Exercises

$ Select a result, outcome or success you would like to have in your life, and then decide upon the one habit that could help most to achieve that goal.

$ Develop the habit of future orientation by thinking and imagining your ideal future in your business or personal life and working toward it.

$ Develop the habit of goal orientation by selecting one main goal, making a plan for its accomplishment, and then working on it every day.

$ Develop the habit of excellence orientation by selecting one key skill that would help you more than any other and then working on becoming better in that area every day.

$ Develop the habit of continuous learning by reading, listening to audio programs, and attending seminars as a normal and natural part of your life.

$ Develop the habit of writing and rewriting your goals in a spiral note-book each morning before you set out.

Action Exercises, continued

$ Develop the habit of action orientation by taking the initiative, by daring to go forward, by moving quickly on opportunities and solving problems.

If you can win complete mastery over self, you will
easily master all else. To triumph over
self is the perfect victory.

—THOMAS À KEMPIS

5

The Habits of People Who Become Millionaires

> The beginning of a habit is like an invisible thread, but every time we repeat the act, we strengthen the strand, add to it another filament, until it becomes a great cable and binds us irrevocably in thought and act.
>
> —ORISON SWETT MARDEN

*Y*OUR GOAL SHOULD BE TO EARN AS much money as you possibly can over the course of your career, to achieve financial independence, and to eventually become a millionaire. This is the most common financial ambition of Americans, and it is eminently achievable if you develop the right habits. Fortunately, becoming a millionaire has never been more possible in all of human history than it is right now, today, here in America, under our economic system.

FIVE MILLION MILLIONAIRES

In the year 1900, there were only 5,000 millionaires in America. By the year 2000, there were more than five million millionaires. In addition, there were decimillionaires, centimillionaires, and more than 300 billionaires and multibillionaires. Almost all of these millionaires and billionaires are first-generation wealth; that is, they began with nothing and accumulated their fortunes in the course of a single working lifetime.

Millionaires come from every conceivable background. Some are well educated, and some are not. Some graduated from the finest universities. Others dropped out of high school. Some came from families that have lived in America for many generations. Others came to America as immigrants with no friends or contacts, no skills, and not even the ability to speak English when they arrived. But they all had one thing in common: they started with nothing and passed the magic million-dollar mark as the result of doing certain things in a certain way, over and over again. They learned and practiced the million-dollar habits that we are explaining throughout this book.

Self-made millionaires have been interviewed and studied exhaustively, hundreds and even thousands of times, both individually and in groups. Some of the very best research on millionaires was conducted by Thomas Stanley and William Danko and summarized in their book *The Millionaire Next Door* (Longstreet Press, 1996), which has gone on to sell almost three million copies.

Every newspaper and magazine seems to have an article or story about one or more men or women who have become financially successful in different fields and occupations as the result of doing certain things in a certain way. And what others have accomplished, you can accomplish as well, if you just learn how.

THINK LIKE A MILLIONAIRE

I wrote earlier, "You become what you think about most of the time." If you sincerely want to be rich, to achieve all your financial goals, and to retire as a self-made millionaire, one of the smartest things you can do is to develop the habits of thinking and acting that have enabled hundreds of thousands—and even millions—of other people to become millionaires.

These habits of financial success are learnable, as all habits are, by practice and repetition.

The first discovery about the thinking patterns of self-made millionaires is that they have the habit of thinking in terms of financial independence most of the time. From an early age or at a certain point in life, they become focused on achieving specific financial goals. They then discipline themselves to make whatever sacrifices are necessary to achieve those goals. They organize and reorganize their entire financial lives—their earning, investing, insuring, and spending activities—in such a way that they are all coordinated and helping them move toward hitting those specific financial targets.

Accumulate or Spend

Most people have the opposite habits with regard to money. Instead of thinking in terms of accumulation, saving, and financial independence, the majority of people think of spending and enjoying every penny they can get their hands on, plus whatever else they can borrow from friends or put on credit cards. In 2002, almost 1.5 million Americans declared personal bankruptcy as the result of borrowing and spending far more than they could ever repay.

At a certain point in life, each person comes to a crossroads. One road leads in the direction of earning, saving, and accumulating, while the other road leads in the direction of earning, spending, and getting into debt. As a fully responsible adult, you must decide which road you are going to take. And no matter what road you have taken up until now, you are free to choose the road that you are going to follow from this day forward.

Take Charge of Your Financial Life

The starting point of achieving financial independence and becoming a self-made millionaire is for you to accept complete responsibility for your financial life. Many people never do this. They instead go through their days, and their money, trusting luck, with the idea that somehow, sometime, someone else will come to the rescue. They buy lottery tickets, gamble, and think about making a killing in the stock market. And they worry about money all the time.

The fact is, serious money is long-term money. Most wealthy people organize their financial lives in such a way that their net worth increases about 8 to 10 percent per year on the amount of money that they have working. They do not look for get-rich-quick schemes or easy money. They are patient, persistent, and farsighted. They discipline themselves to save and accumulate money over many years. They do not speculate, take risks, or look for fast ways to make money quickly and easily. As a result of these habitual ways of thinking about their money, each year their wealth grows. Eventually, they pass the million-dollar mark and usually keep on going.

Develop a Millionaire Mindset

Business philosopher Jim Rohn once wrote,

> *Becoming a millionaire is not that difficult, but it is not the most important thing. The most important part of becoming a millionaire is the person that you have to become to accumulate a million dollars in the first place.*

This is a wonderful insight. In order to become wealthy, you must develop a completely different mindset from the average person who worries about money most of his life. You must develop a completely different character, personality, and set of habits if you are to achieve your financial goals and then hold onto the money.

My financial advisor once told me, "The first million is extremely difficult to acquire, but the second million is almost inevitable."

When you become the kind of person who can earn and accumulate a million dollars or more, you will also be the kind of person who can earn the second and third million as well. Even if something unfortunate happens, and you lose all your money, you could make it back again fairly quickly because you would have become the kind of person who can become a millionaire. And once you become that kind of person, you never lose the ability.

THE FIRST HABIT OF MILLIONAIRES

Perhaps the most easily identifiable habit of self-made millionaires is the habit of frugality. Wealthy people are careful with every penny and every dollar. They allocate their funds carefully and with great deliberation. They never buy new when they can buy used. They never buy if they can lease, and they never lease if they can rent. They never rent or lease if they can borrow. They know that, as the English saying goes, "If you take care of your pennies, the pounds will take care of themselves."

For example, most self-made millionaires do not buy new cars. They wait until a good quality car is about two years old before they buy it. Even then, they have the car thoroughly checked out by a reputable mechanic. Once they feel confident that it is an excellent buy, in good condition, they buy the car and then drive it for five or ten years before replacing it.

Most new cars drop 20 percent in value as soon as you drive them off the lot. After two years, many cars have lost 30 to 50 percent of their value. They are still in excellent condition and often still covered by factory warranties. When you buy a good-quality used car, you can save many thousands of dollars, all of which can be invested and allowed to grow at compound interest toward your ultimate goal of financial independence.

SAVE YOUR MONEY

Self-made millionaires develop the habit of regular saving and investment from an early age. As multimillionaire W. Clement Stone once wrote, "If you cannot save money, the seeds of greatness are not in you."

George Classon, in his best seller, *The Richest Man In Babylon* (Signet reissue, 2002), wrote that the key to financial success is to "pay yourself first." He recommends that you save at least 10 percent of your income, off the top, before any other expenditure, for the entirety of your working life.

Human beings are creatures of habit. We very quickly adapt to almost any external condition or circumstance. If you save 10 percent off the top of your paycheck and discipline yourself to live on the other 90 percent, you will soon adjust your lifestyle downward slightly so that you are quite comfortable on the lesser amount. In no time at all, living at this level becomes a habit, and you stop thinking about it.

Many people are deeply in debt, and the idea of saving 10 percent of their income, off the top of each paycheck, is too difficult for them even to consider. In this case, which is quite common, I recommend a gradual process where you begin by saving 1 percent of your income and living on the other 99 percent.

For example, if you are earning $2,000 per month, make a decision today to save $20 per month, or 67 cents per day. You can then live on the other $1,980.

Go down to the bank and open up a separate account, your "financial independence" account. Money that goes into this account flows only one way—inward. Once you put money into this savings/investment account, you never, ever take it out or spend it for any reason. It has only one purpose: to enable you to achieve financial independence as soon as possible.

Once you have become comfortable living on 99 percent of your income, increase your monthly savings rate to 2 percent off the top. Within one year, you will find yourself living quite comfortably on 10 percent of your current income. Continue this process until you are saving 15 percent and then 20 percent of your income, off the top. You will not even notice the difference in your standard of living because it will be so gradual. But the difference in your financial life will be absolutely extraordinary.

Take Complete Control of Your Financial Life

By developing the habit of thinking more carefully about your income and savings, you will soon find yourself spending less and less on your day-to-day expenses. You will find yourself paying down your debts and not incurring new debts. You will find yourself delaying or deferring expenditures and finally not even buying those items at all.

Meanwhile, the habit of saving money out of every paycheck will cause your financial fortress account to grow. In a year, you will have a few hundred dollars. In a couple of years, you will have a few thousand dollars. In 10 to 20 years, you will have several hundred thousand dollars.

As your financial accumulation account grows, develop the habit of adding every additional, unexpected amount of money that comes to you to this account, to make it grow faster. If you sell something from around the house, get a bonus at work, or receive an income tax refund, instead of spending it immediately, as unsuccessful people do, instead put it into your financial fortress account.

Activate the Law of Attraction

Here is an extraordinary discovery. When you begin to save money and you feel positive and happy about your growing account, these positive emotions imbue that money with a form of energy that begins to attract more money into your life, and into that account. Old friends will pay back debts you had forgotten a long time ago. You will have opportunities to earn additional amounts of money that had not occurred to you. You will sell things that you had kept for a long time and thought had no value. And as you add these amounts to your account, your account will develop even more positive energy and attract even larger amounts of money.

I had heard about this concept for many years, but I was always broke and there never seemed to be anything I could do about it. Then, about two years after I got married and started my own business, I ran out of money. I had been able to buy a house with my life savings, but now I had to sell the house to get cash.

We moved to a rented house, and at that point, my wife, Barbara, demanded that I turn over to her $10,000 from the proceeds from the sale of the house. After some arguing, I gave in. She took the money and deposited it in another bank account to which I did not have access. No matter how many financial problems we had in the months ahead, she refused to even consider the possibility of spending that money. This was her security blanket.

The most remarkable thing happened. From that day forward, we were never broke again. Even though it was the midst of a recession and businesses were going bankrupt all around us, we were never again out of money. Every week, every month, business came in, the bills were paid, opportunities opened up, and exciting possibilities seemed to be attracted into our lives. Within a couple of years, we were able to move out of the rented house and buy a beautiful new home in a lovely neighborhood. Two years later, we were able to buy a home that cost five times as much on a beautiful golf course, overlooking two lakes with the ocean in the distance.

Learn to Love Saving Your Money

In Chapter 1, we described habits as "conditioned responses to stimuli." With regard to this definition, there is a special habit that financially successful people learn or develop over time. It is the habit of responding to incoming money in a particular way.

When we are growing up, we are encouraged to save money from our allowances. However, as children, we look upon money as a tool with which to buy candy, toys, and other things that make us happy. As a result, we naturally begin to look upon saving as a punishment, something that hurts us and deprives us of the candy, toys, and enjoyable things we desire. At an early age, most people begin to associate savings with pain, with sacrifice, with loss of pleasure, satisfaction, and happiness.

As adults, this negative habit is manifested in our desire to spend money as soon as we make it. Many people in their late teens and 20s look upon every paycheck as an opportunity to go out and spend as much money as they can. This is why it is generally known in the restaurant business that the dining rooms will be the fullest at the middle and end of each month, on paydays.

People very early begin to associate spending with happiness and saving with pain. Since the basic human motivation is to move away from pain toward pleasure, from discomfort toward comfort, and from dissatisfaction toward satisfaction, most people develop the habit of associating spending with enjoyment and saving with unhappiness.

Rewire Your Thinking

Your job is to reverse the wiring on this habit. It is to detach the wires from one set of attitudes and reattach them with a different set of attitudes. Your job is to begin thinking in terms of pleasure whenever you think of saving and accumulation and pain whenever you think of spending and getting rid of your money.

The Law of Emotion says, "Whichever emotion you dwell upon will grow, just as a fire would if you put more fuel upon it." The more you think about the pleasure and enjoyment that you get from seeing your financial fortress account growing, the more motivated you will be to spend less, save more, and grow that account. In no time at all, at the end of each month, instead of worrying about the amount of money you have relative to your bills and payments, you will instead be reviewing the amount of money that is accumulating in your bank account.

Most people who become financially successful develop the habit of thinking in terms of the pleasure and satisfaction they get from saving, investing, and growing their money. Most financial failures, on the other hand, get most of their pleasure out of thinking of ways they can spend their money as quickly as they acquire it.

LOOK RICH OR BE RICH

Stanley and Danko, in *The Millionaire Next Door*, explain that most self-made millionaires drive used cars, live in average neighborhoods, wear average priced clothes and watches, and are very careful with their money. In addition, very few of them buy boats, recreational vehicles, second homes, personal airplanes, or invest in expensive vacations. Stanley and Danko point out that there are "Those who look rich, and those who are rich." Your job is to be one of those people who are genuinely rich, rather than a person who spends a lot of money but has very little in the bank.

Truly wealthy people develop the habit of "getting rich slow" rather than "getting rich quick." To assure this, they have two rules with regard to money. Rule number one: Don't lose money. Rule number two: If ever you feel tempted, refer back to rule number one, "don't lose money."

People who become wealthy spend much more time thinking about their finances than people who remain poor. The average adult spends two to three hours each month studying and thinking about money, usually at bill-paying time. The average self-made millionaire, by contrast, spends 20 to 30 hours per month thinking, studying, and planning finances. Since the very act of focusing on your money will dramatically improve the decisions you make with regard to it, people who invest more time planning their finances invariably make better decisions and get better results.

PRACTICE WEDGE THEORY TO BECOME RICH

Here is an excellent technique that I teach in my "Financial Success Seminars." It is what I call the "Wedge Theory." It is guaranteed to make you financially independent faster than you can even imagine.

Parkinson's Law, developed by author C. Northcote Parkinson, says, "Expenses rise to meet income." This means that, because your income increases gradually, your expenditures increase gradually as well to match your income. No matter how much money you make, your expenses eventually rise to consume it all, and a little bit more besides. Over time, you develop the habit of always spending whatever you earn or receive.

Sometimes I ask my audiences this question, "If I could wave a magic wand and double or triple your income, would that solve your financial problems?"

Then I wait and watch their faces. Almost immediately, people raise their hands, smile, and nod. They all agree that if they could double or triple their current incomes, that would solve all their financial problems.

Then I ask a follow-up question, "Going back to what you earned in your first job, is there anyone here who has already doubled or tripled their income?"

After a short pause, virtually everyone in the audience raises their hands. All have already doubled and tripled their incomes from their first jobs. Many have increased their incomes five and ten times from the first job they took when they left school. And it hasn't done a bit of good. They still have financial problems because they have become subject to Parkinson's Law, "Expenses rise to meet income."

Save Half of Your Future Increases

Here is how the Wedge Theory works. When you ask a person to save a certain amount of their current income, they will almost always agree that it is a good idea, but they will also claim that it is not possible. To save out of your current income will mean reducing your standard of living. It may mean moving to a smaller place, driving a smaller car, eating cheaper foods, or not going out as often. Because human beings are creatures of habit, even if they can mentally agree that saving is a good idea, the actual reduction in living standards that it requires is so unacceptable that they are not able to discipline themselves to take the first step.

In Wedge Theory, it is different. Instead of cutting back on your current lifestyle, you resolve to save 50 percent of every increase you receive from your work from this day forward. This is something you can do because you don't yet have the money built into your daily way of life. It is much easier for people to commit to saving money that they have not yet received than it is to get people to agree to save money by cutting back on their current standard of living.

By practicing some of the other techniques and methods taught later on in this book, you will be able to increase your income by 5 percent, 10 percent, and even 25 percent per year. To become wealthy, you must develop the habit, starting today, of saving fully 50 percent of these future increases. You can still spend the other 50 percent on whatever you like, but you must agree to save half of the money that you don't even have yet. This should not be hard for you.

Depending upon your age, and the rate at which your income grows, saving 50 percent of your increases in the years ahead will soon allow you to acquire an enormous amount of money. And the more money you acquire, the more money you will attract to yourself. By disciplining yourself and developing the habit of saving half of your increase for the rest of your career, you will pay off all your debts, build an enormous financial fortress, and eventually become financially independent.

DEVELOP THE HABITS OF WEALTHY PEOPLE

With regard to your growing bank account, millionaires develop a series of other habits to assure that they don't lose money, and that their money grows steadily over time. One of the best habits you can develop is the habit of getting good financial advice before you do anything with your growing account. Ask around and find a financial advisor who has already become financially successful by investing his or her personal money in the areas that he or she recommends to you. Your ability to choose excellent financial advisors can be the critical factor in making good investment decisions.

Develop the habit of investigating before you invest in anything. The rule is, "Spend as much time investigating the investment as you spend earning the money that you are thinking of investing."

Fast financial decisions are usually poor financial decisions. Develop the habit of taking your time, of moving slowly, of finding out every detail of the business or investment before you ever think of writing a check. Never allow anyone to pressure you into an investment decision. Never allow yourself to feel that a financial investment decision is urgent and must be made immediately. A wealthy man I worked for once told me, "Investments are like buses; there will always be another one coming along."

Sometimes, the best investments are the ones you never make at all. Make a habit of thoroughly understanding the investment before you ever think of parting with your hard-earned money. If there is anything that you do not understand or which seems too complicated for you, do not put your money in that area at all.

Warren Buffet, one of the richest men in the world as the result of his investing acumen, refused to invest in any of the high-tech or dotcom companies during the boom of the 1990s. Everyone accused him of being out of step and old fashioned. He simply replied, "I don't understand these businesses and therefore, I will not put any of my money into them." He turned out to be right, and all the others turned out to be wrong.

Never Trust Luck

An important habit for financial success is the habit of insuring properly against any risk that you cannot write a check to cover. It is amazing how many people have spent years accumulating money and then lost it all because they did not have proper insurance policies in place. Develop the habit of using what I call "worst possible option" (WPO) thinking. Always ask yourself, "What is the worst possible thing that could happen in this situation?"

Whatever it is, make provisions to ensure or guard against it. Never trust to luck.

Hope is not a strategy. Wishing is not a strategy. Only careful planning, organizing, and insuring constitute a strategy for your financial life.

Be sure that you have sufficient life insurance to cover your family and all their financial needs if something should happen to you. Be sure that you have adequate fire and damage insurance for your home. Check and upgrade your policies on a regular basis to make sure that they cover "replacement value." Insure your automobiles for damage and liability. Be sure to have adequate health insurance that covers you for any emergency and for long-term care.

No one likes to spend money on insurance, but it is one of the smartest things that you can possibly do on your road to financial independence. By insuring properly, you will never be caught off guard by an unexpected accident or emergency. An additional benefit of being fully insured is that it gives you a feeling of calm confidence that allows you to think more clearly and be much more effective in everything else you do.

Cover Your Assets

As you begin to accumulate money, develop the habit of protecting your estate from unnecessary taxes and frivolous lawsuits. Invest in the services of a lawyer who specializes in wills and estate planning. Set up a family limited partnership under the direction of a good lawyer and transfer your assets into the partnership so they cannot be seized in a lawsuit or taxed away if something were to happen to you. As the old saying goes, "A stitch in time saves nine." Small actions that you take in planning, investigating, and insuring your assets can save you an enormous amount of money on your road to financial independence.

Do Your Homework

In addition to the habits discussed above, another important habit that wealthy people develop is the habit of carefully considering every expenditure before they make it. This involves getting as much information as possible on the various prices and costs involved in any financial decision. The power is always on the side of the person with the best information.

Develop the habit of negotiating more effectively to get higher prices when you sell and lower prices when you buy. A good negotiator can save or gain 10 percent, 20 percent, and more on every financial transaction. Each dollar saved or gained is additional money that you can put away to accumulate and grow in your financial fortress account.

Develop the habit of asking for higher prices when you are selling and asking for lower prices when you buy. Ask for lower interest rates. Ask for better terms and conditions. Ask for immediate payment when you sell and ask for deferred payment when you buy. Ask repeatedly. Ask pleasantly. Ask courteously. Ask expectantly. Ask confidently. But don't be afraid to ask. Ask for what you want, and if you don't get it, ask for something else.

GET RICH SLOWLY

When people make a lot of money quickly, as the result of success in the stock market, a business breakthrough, a show business success, or an invention, the story gets into the newspapers and magazines. But this is precisely because great financial success in a short time is so unusual.

Most great fortunes are built slowly. They are based on the principle of compound interest, what Albert Einstein called, "The greatest power in the universe." In fully 99 percent of cases where people become wealthy, it is over a long period of time, and it is based on slow, incremental growth as the result of compound interest.

Every dollar that you save, properly invested and protected, has the ability to grow 5 to 10 percent each year. As your money grows, it compounds on itself, and grows even more. According to Stanley and Danko, it takes the average millionaire 22 years to accumulate a million dollars from the time he gets serious about his financial life. They get rich slowly, by gradually increasing their earning ability, saving more and more from their income, and investing it carefully and intelligently so that it grows and compounds over the years. You must do the same.

THE PURSUIT OF HAPPINESS

The philosopher Aristotle concluded, in his Nicomachaen Ethics, "The ultimate end or purpose of all human life is the achievement of personal happiness."

Becoming financially independent as the result of developing million-dollar habits is a great goal in itself, but it is not the most important thing. It is the person you must become, in terms of courage, character, thoughtfulness, and persistence, that is most important. As the result of becoming financially successful over a long period of time, you will feel truly happy and satisfied with yourself, and with every other part of your life.

This is the most worthwhile goal of all.

Action Exercises

$ Make a decision today that you are going to accumulate more than a million dollars in the years ahead. Write it down as a goal, make a plan, and then do something toward achieving it every single day.

$ Conduct a complete financial analysis on your life; determine your net worth, your income and expenses, and your future possibilities.

$ Open a special financial fortress account and begin putting money into it at every opportunity; never spend this money on anything except investing and growth.

$ Get your financial life organized, with proper estate planning and insurance, with a family limited partnership to protect your assets.

Action Exercises, *continued*

$ Begin saving a fixed percentage of your income each month. Practice the Wedge Theory and save 50 percent of every increase from this day forward.

$ Investigate before you invest; learn every detail of the business, and be sure you thoroughly understand how your money is to be used and how it will be returned.

$ Practice frugality in all expenditures. Never buy new if you can buy used, never pay full price if you can negotiate something cheaper, delay all major expenditures until you have had ample time to think about them.

Go out and buy yourself a five-cent pencil and
a ten-cent notebook and begin to write down
some million dollar ideas for yourself.

—BOB GRINDE

6

The Habits That Get You Paid More and Promoted Faster

> The individual who wants to reach the top in business must appreciate the might of the force of habit—and must understand that practices are what create habits. He must be quick to break those habits that can break him—and hasten to adopt those practices that will become the habits that help him achieve the success he desires.
>
> —JOHN PAUL GETTY

*C*ONFUCIUS ONCE WROTE, "HE WHO would rule must learn to obey." The most successful executives, entrepreneurs, and managers are usually excellent as employees on their way up. They learn or develop the habits that enable them to make a significant, valuable contribution to their companies and organizations, and as a result, they get paid more and promoted faster than the people around them. This should be your goal as well.

Most self-made millionaires are entrepreneurs who start and build their own successful businesses. But many self-made millionaires are salespeople and executives of successful businesses who do an excellent job, make an excellent contribution, and get paid extremely well, both in the form of cash and stock.

Only about 1 percent of the population has the temperament and combination of abilities necessary for successful entrepreneurship. But fully 99 percent of the population has the ability to work well in a specific job or occupation. Because most people spend 95 percent of their life working for someone else, it is absolutely essential that you learn how to make yourself valuable—and then indispensable. This is the key to your success at work.

YOUR CHOICES ARE UNLIMITED

More than 100,000 different jobs and job categories exist in the United States alone. There are an unlimited number of things that you can do to earn a good living and to achieve financial independence. You must therefore develop the habit of thinking about the work that you would most love to do. Instead of accepting whatever job or position comes along, you should be continually thinking about your ideal job, exactly as if you could design it personally in every respect.

The highest paid and most successful people in our society do what they love to do as much of the time as they possibly can. You should continually be standing back, examining yourself objectively, and then practicing the habit of focusing on your special talents and abilities.

Each person is born with the ability to do one or more things in an exceptional fashion. Just as you have multiple intelligences, you have multiple abilities as well. You will only really be happy and successful when you find the kind of work that taps into the unique talents you have today, or which you can develop tomorrow.

The Ideal Job for You

Dr. Victor Frankl, the founder of Logotherapy, wrote that there are four types of jobs that you can do. The first of these jobs are hard to learn and hard to do. This type of work would include a task like accounting or bookkeeping for a person who has no natural skill in that area. It would be hard to learn, and no matter how many years you did it, it would be hard to do. Many people find themselves in jobs or careers where they are mismatched in terms of their natural abilities and what the job requires. Their work is always hard and seldom satisfying. Don't let this happen to you.

The second type of job Frankl identifies is a job that is hard to learn but easy to do. This may be a skill like typing or flying an airplane. It takes tremendous dedication and concentration to learn, but once you have mastered it, it is quite easy to do, hour after hour. Unfortunately, this type of job can become boring and unchallenging over time. It seldom causes you to stretch your capabilities and grow your talents.

The third type of job you might find yourself in is a job that is easy to learn but hard to do. Physical labor falls into this category, like digging a ditch. It's often easy to learn to do a physically difficult job, but it is always hard to do, no matter how long you do it. Think about chopping wood!

The fourth job category, and the most important, are those tasks that you find easy to learn and easy to do. You learned it so easily and do it so naturally that you almost forget when and how you learned it in the first place.

As you can imagine, the jobs and tasks that are easy to learn and easy to do are the best indicators of your natural talents and abilities. This is where you are the most likely to do the best job, get the best results, and be paid the very most. Throughout your life and career, you must be continually analyzing your activities to identify the things that you learn and do easily and from which you get the best results and rewards. This type of work is the key to career success.

Focus on Contribution

Even if you are running your own business, as we teach in our Entrepreneurial Coaching Programs, your most important responsibility to yourself is to identify the few things that you do the most easily, that you enjoy, and that make the greatest contribution to your work or to your company. Your job is then to organize your workday and your work life so that you spend more and more time doing more of the things you do best and get the best results. This is the key to entrepreneurial success.

The fact is, the quality of your thinking determines the quality of your life. The more time you spend thinking about who you are—in terms of your natural talents and abilities and what you most want from your work—the better decisions you will make and the more you will accomplish. This way of thinking is essential in your choices of a job, a boss, an industry, and a career.

Before you take your first job, or when you change jobs in the course of your career, stop for a moment and draw a line under the past. Imagine that you are starting over, with all the knowledge and skill that you have accumulated to this date. Look around you at all the opportunities that are open to you, and then take your time in choosing the right job or business for you at your current level of knowledge, skill, and development. Invest your time and your life carefully. They are all you've got, and they are irreplaceable.

Seek Opportunity Versus Security

People are always asking me how they can make more money in their current jobs. I ask them what sort of jobs they do and what sort of companies they work for. They often tell me they are working in an industry where sales are flat or declining or that they are working for a company that is not growing. Sometimes they are doing a job where the pay is largely fixed and in which there are few opportunities for advancement or higher income. In these cases, I have to tell them they are in a situation with a limited future and only an unsatisfactory present.

Look around you in the current job market. What are the businesses and industries that are growing in sales and popularity? What are the products and services that are selling well? What companies have increasing profits and rising stock prices? What states or regions of the country have the most companies and industries that seem to be prospering?

If you sincerely want to become a millionaire over the course of your lifetime, you must be prepared to make important changes, including moving geographically from one part of the country to another if necessary. You must be prepared to leave a job or industry if the prospects for that industry are declining. You must be honest with yourself.

Many people have totally changed their lives, dramatically increased their incomes, put their careers onto the fast track, and moved rapidly toward financial independence by making major changes in where they were working or what they were doing.

Ignore the Past and Focus on the Future

There is a concept in accounting called a "sunk cost." These are defined as money that has been spent and cannot be recouped. They are funds that are gone forever in a company or business, like last year's advertising. They cannot be retrieved. They have no value. They are sunk, as in a deep ocean.

You have sunk costs in your career as well. You may have invested weeks, months, and even years in getting an education or acquiring experience in a particular field. But the market has changed, and there may be no demand for what you are capable of doing. No one is willing to hire you or pay you very much to do it.

Many people have invested an enormous amount of time and money in the development of talents and skills for which there is no existing or future market. But they have a hard time facing this fact, or admitting it to themselves or others.

Practice Zero-Based Thinking Regularly

One of the most important habits you can develop is the habit of "zero-based thinking." In zero-based thinking, you put every one of your previous decisions on trial for its life on a regular basis. You ask this question, "Is there anything that I am doing today that, knowing what I now know, I wouldn't get into again if I had to do it over?"

Apply this question to every part of your life—especially to your job, position, career, and current situation. If you were not doing what you are currently doing, would you get into it again today, knowing what you now know about this area? Asking and answering this question takes a good deal of courage.

The fact is, in a world of rapid change, you will always have situations that, with your current knowledge, you wouldn't get into again today if you had the choice. These situations will almost always be the primary causes of stress or dissatisfaction in your life. They will cause you the most aggravation and frustration. If you stay in a zero-based situation long enough, it can even make you physically ill.

If the answer to this question, "Is there anything that I'm doing that I wouldn't get into again today?" is "yes," then your next question should be, "How do I get out of this situation and how fast?"

Often you can change your entire life by simply having the courage to face up to the fact that your previous decision has not turned out to be as good as you originally thought it would be. There is nothing wrong with this. You are not perfect. Everyone makes decisions they later regret. This will happen throughout your life. The only question is, "How long are you going to stay in a situation that you know is not right for you?" It is not possible for you to be successful and happy in your career or job if, knowing what you now know, you wouldn't even get into it today if you had it to do over.

GETTING THE IDEAL JOB FOR YOU

Once you have decided what you most enjoy doing, what you have the potential to do extremely well, the part of the country where you would like to live, and the type of business you would like to work in, the next step is to begin the process of "informational interviewing." Instead of applying for a job in a particular company, you merely seek information about what is going on in that company and industry. You can even position or imagine yourself as a reporter in the process of gathering information to write a story.

You begin your search by calling up a decision maker in a company in an industry that interests you and saying something like this, "I am doing some research on this business (or industry) and I would very much like to get a few minutes of your time to ask you how you see your business evolving and developing in the future."

You will be amazed at how open people are to talk to you about their company or business. After you have spoken to people in several companies, you will have assembled an excellent information base that will enable you to determine first, whether you want to work in that industry, and second, which particular company you would like to work for.

Many years ago, new in town and with no experience in the business, I conducted this process with the top four companies in the industry. Within one month, I received job offers from all four companies and accepted the one with the best reputation and the toughest hiring standards. This method really works!

Remember, your time is your life. Choose your job with care. You are going to be exchanging a certain amount of your life for that job, and your time is more important than the money that you will receive. Money can be replaced, but time spent is gone forever.

Take the Time to Choose Well

In taking a new job, choose your boss with care. One of the fastest ways to move ahead rapidly in your career is to work for an excellent boss. An excellent boss is invariably someone who is competent and capable, positive and constructive, and under whom you can learn and grow at a rapid rate. Most successful people can tell you of bosses that became key factors in their subsequent success.

On the other hand, some people fall into the habit of taking whatever job is offered to them when they need a job and working for whichever boss they happen to get. They take whatever work assignments are given to them and accept whatever hours or working conditions are offered. Instead of being self-reliant and self-determined, they become reactive and accepting. Instead of seeing themselves as responsible and in charge of their own careers, they begin to see themselves as passive agents, merely doing what they are told to do. This is definitely not for you.

TWO HABITS FOR RAPID ADVANCEMENT

Over the years, I have been invited to speak to graduating classes of business students. They invariably ask me for advice on how to get ahead in the world of work. I will tell you what I tell them.

You can develop two habits to help you get ahead faster than any "success secrets" you will ever learn. These habits will serve you well as an employee, as a manager or executive, or as an entrepreneur and business owner. They are simple, easy to learn, and incredibly powerful.

HABIT ONE

Remember that the normal hours of work are simply averages, and they are for average employee. They have nothing to do with you.

If the workday starts at 8:30, you should be at work and busy by 8 o'clock. You should work steadily all day long. If the workday ends at 5 o'clock, you should continue working until 5:30 or 6:00, or even later. The simple act of starting earlier, working harder, and staying later, will increase your productivity by anything from 50 to 100 percent. The people who are in the best position to help you get ahead will soon notice these work habits. They will give you an edge over any of your co-workers.

HABIT TWO

As soon as you feel that you are on top of your work, go to your boss and say you want "more responsibility." Say you very much like your job and you want to make an even more valuable contribution to the company. You are not asking for more money or for special recognition, you simply want more responsibility.

Fast-Tracking My Career

Many years ago, I went to work for a large company with about 200 employees. I was the low man on the totem pole. I was stuck in a tiny office in the back with a desk, a chair, and no pictures on the wall. I was given a variety of small tasks that changed from week to week.

Feeling a little frustrated after a couple of weeks of this, I went to my boss, the chairman of the company, and told him I was caught up with my work and wanted more responsibility. The fact is, I like to work, and I was bored. I wanted to be busier and more active. My desire for more responsibility was perfectly selfish.

I remember my boss nodded and smiled and told me he would think about it. But nothing happened. Therefore, every couple of days, when I met with my boss, I would end the conversation by saying, "By the way, I would really like more work to do, more responsibility."

Finally, about two weeks after I began this campaign, my boss asked me if I would take care of something for him that was outside of my basic job description. I thanked him heartily, took the task back to my office, and began work on it.

And I developed a habit that changed my life. As soon as I received the additional responsibility I had been asking for, I developed the habit of doing the job quickly and well. I got it done fast. I worked late into the night and over the weekend to get this job finished in an excellent fashion and get it back to my boss.

He had given me the additional responsibility on a Friday afternoon. By Monday morning, I had it completed and typed up so it was on his desk when he arrived that day. Later on, in passing, he mentioned he hadn't needed it done immediately, but he thanked me for getting it done so quickly.

Keep Asking for More

Later that week, he complimented me once more on how well and how quickly the job had been done. I used this as an opportunity to immediately ask for more responsibility. Soon he gave me another job, and then another, and then another. In every case, whatever he gave me to do, I grabbed it like a fumble in a football game and ran for yards. I took the job and immediately went to work on it, completing it quickly, and getting it back to him long before he needed it. This did not go unnoticed.

In addition, I began observing some of the tasks that took up his time, and without asking, I began working on them and completing them as well, so they were done when he got in. I answered correspondence, dealt with client service problems, visited customers, and gathered information to save him time. This did not go unnoticed either.

Your Chance Will Come

Then one day, a major project came up. He asked me if I was interested in taking charge of it. It was in an area where I had never worked before, but I immediately agreed. I then threw my whole heart into doing the job quickly and well.

After that, I was given another project, and then another, and then still another. By the end of one year, I had three divisions of the company working under me. I had moved into the second largest office in the building and had a staff of 23 people. I was operating businesses that were generating many millions of dollars in sales and profitability.

By developing the reputation as being the "go-to guy" in the company, the one who got things done faster and better than anyone else, my star rose and rose and rose. My income doubled and tripled. I received bonuses and special incentives that enabled me to buy a new house and a Mercedes.

Some time later, I was hired away by the president of another major corporation at triple what I was earning in my current job. I later learned that my former boss had ended up paying me more in salaries and bonuses than he had ever paid an employee in the course of his 25-year career. And I earned every penny of it by asking for more responsibility and then getting the job done quickly and well. You can do the same.

TAKE INITIATIVE AND GET THE JOB DONE FAST

Remember I talked about the importance of the qualities of action orientation and taking initiative. In every job, in every area, in every field, these qualities cause you to stand out favorably from everyone else around you.

Whether you work for someone else or you run your own business, the qualities of taking responsibility and getting the job done fast will do more to help you get paid more and promoted faster than any other two habits you can develop.

In Larry Bossidy's best selling book *Execution* (Crown Publishing, 2002), based on his many years of running Fortune 500 corporations, he writes that the most valuable people he has ever met in business are those rare few who have developed the habit of fulfilling their responsibilities and getting the job they were hired to do done. In every study of successful people in business, this single characteristic seems to stand out. All successful people, in any job, in any organization, are those who take responsibility and move quickly to fulfill those responsibilities and get the results required of them. In business, results are everything.

Don't Waste Time

One of the most important habits you can develop, which will help you in any job, is the habit of working all the time you work.

According to Robert Half International, the average employee works only 50 percent of the time. The other 50 percent of working time is largely wasted. It is spent in idle chitchat and conversation with co-workers, late arrivals, extended coffee breaks and lunches, and early departures. It is dribbled away making private phone calls, reading the newspaper, taking care of personal business, and surfing the Internet. Only 50 percent of the time for which the average person is paid is actually spent on work-related activities.

Even worse, when the average employee is actually working, he or she does the tasks that are fun and easy rather than the jobs that are hard and important. Most people "major in minors" and work on low priority activities. When you discipline yourself to focus on high priority tasks and make every minute count, you will immediately separate yourself from everyone else and take full control of your career and your future.

Resolve to work all the time you work. Start a little earlier, and when you get in, go to work immediately. If someone wants to talk to you, say you would like to chat but not right now. Right now, you have to get *back to work*!

Keep repeating to yourself the mantra, "Back to work! Back to work! Back to work!" Tell your co-workers that you can socialize with them after work, if you have the time. And then get back to work.

Be a Hard Worker

Imagine that a management-consulting firm is going to come into your company and do a survey one year from today. In this survey, they are going to ask everyone in the company to rank everyone else in the company in terms of who works the hardest, all the way down to who works the least hard. Imagine that your goal is to come out on the top of this survey. Every single day you are at work, imagine that you are being watched with hidden cameras. At the end of the month or the year, a vote is going to be taken on the hardest-working person in the company. Your job is to be sure you win this vote.

Nothing will bring you to the attention of people who can help you faster than developing a habit for hard, hard work. In every study of successful people, whether they are athletes, executives, entrepreneurs, or self-made millionaires in any field, the most obvious habit they have is that they work much longer and harder than their co-workers.

Join the Elite

There have been many studies about wealth and poverty in the United States and worldwide. These studies try to explain income distribution and are often used as the basis for welfare payments, unemployment compensation, and levels of taxation.

Again and again, these studies show that the highest paid people in America work about 60 hours a week. The lowest paid people in America, the ones at the poverty line, work fewer than 25 hours per week. The highest paid households in America have two or more people who work long, hard hours. The most impoverished households in America are those with perhaps one wage earner who works only a few hours per week.

There is a direct relationship between how hard you work and how much you are paid. There is a direct relationship between how hard you work and how rapidly you are promoted. There is a direct relationship between how hard you work and the value of the contribution you make to your company. People who work longer hours are invariably more valuable, paid more, and promoted faster than people who do not.

THE KEY TO CAREER SUCCESS

Andrew Grove, the chairman of Intel, was interviewed in *Fortune* magazine some time ago and asked what he felt had been the biggest changes that had taken place in the world of work in the past decade. He answered, "In my estimation, the two most important changes were these: First of all, every person today is now the architect of his or her own career. Each person has to see himself or herself as completely responsible for everything that happens to them, especially for their own work habits, and their own training and development. No one could rely on a company taking care of them throughout their careers."

His second observation was even more important. He said that today, the key to success in any job is to "add value." At one time, you could get a job, reach a certain level of accomplishment, and then coast for months and even years on your previous achievements. Today, however, you must be looking for ways to add value every single day. Your company no longer cares what you might have accomplished in the past. The main question today is, "What have you done for me lately?"

Gary Hamel and C. K. Prahaled, two of the top strategic planners in the world today, in their book *Competing for the Future* (Harvard Business School Press, 1994), write that a company's key to competitive advantage is to project forward five years and identify the core competencies and skills it will be need to be a market leader at that time.

By the same token, one of the most important habits you can develop is the habit of looking forward three to five years and identifying the additional skills and competencies you will need to be at the top of your field at that time. What are the trends in your industry? What are the skills possessed by the highest paid people in your industry today? Where is your industry going, and what will you have to be absolutely excellent at doing three to five years from now if you want to earn an excellent income? These are the key questions that determine the direction of your career.

The Race Is On

Management writer and guru Peter Drucker writes that, "The only skill that will be important in the 21st century is the skill of learning new skills. Everything else will become obsolete over time."

It has been said often that, "Whatever got you to where you are today is not enough to keep you there." Management author Tom Peters says, "Whatever you are doing well today, you will have to be doing it vastly better one year from today if you want to keep your current position." The race is on, and you are in it.

Continually look for ways to add value, to contribute more than you are contributing today. Never forget that you are a "knowledge worker," and the value of your work is not determined by the hours that you put in, but by the results that you get out.

Make a habit of focusing on the most important and valuable results you can accomplish in your position. Keep looking forward and identifying the additional skills and abilities you can develop to enable you to add more value by getting even better and more important results. This is the way to put yourself on the side of the angels and to put your career onto the fast track.

LOOK LIKE A WINNER

One of the most important million-dollar habit you can develop, which can have an inordinate effect on how fast you move onward and upward, has to do with your personal appearance and image. You must develop the habit of dressing like a person who is going somewhere in life.

Human beings are intensely visual. We are inordinately influenced by the external appearance of other people. Some surveys suggest that we form our first impression in the first four seconds of meeting a person and finalize our conclusions about that person in the first 30 seconds. After we have made a judgment and come to a conclusion about a person, our mind then strives to justify the decision we have already made. Something quite abrupt or shocking has to occur for us to alter our first impression. This is the way our minds work.

Sometimes people say, "People should not judge me by the way I look on the outside." This is a nice idea, but the fact is that you judge everyone you meet by the way they look on the outside, usually within 30 seconds.

One of the rules for success is that "Everything counts!" Everything helps or hurts. Everything adds up or takes away. Everything is either moving you toward a goal of your own choosing or moving you away from that goal. Everything counts! This rule is as applicable in the way you look as in any other area.

In the image that you project, everything counts as well. If it doesn't help, it hurts. One of the smartest things you can do is purchase a couple of books on personal image and then select your clothes, your grooming, your makeup, and your accessories so that you look like the kind of person who is competent, efficient, and trustworthy.

Human beings tend to be incredibly perceptive. And we are very much influenced by the external appearance of a person. When you take the time and effort to dress well and to look the part of a capable person, you open doors for yourself that might otherwise remain closed to you.

What Every Company Wants

Business owners and executives want to be proud of their staff. Many people work hard and do a good job but are passed over for promotion, year after year, because of their external appearance. They are often overweight and unkempt. Their hair is too long or poorly cared for. Their clothes and accessories are ill fitting and do not go with their other clothes. Their shoes are unpolished or mismatched to their clothes or position. As a result, the people around them, especially their superiors, immediately discount their value and ignore their opinions.

In Chapters 7 and 8, we will talk about building a business and about sales and marketing. In those chapters, I will explain the importance of positioning and branding in selling a product or service. Both of these concepts are applicable to you personally and in your work life as well.

Here's an exercise for you. Imagine taking a picture of yourself as you show up for work in the course of the week. Imagine circulating that picture to others and asking the question, "What kind of a person is this?"

How would people who don't know you describe you after looking at a photograph of you the way you normally appear at work? Would they say, "This is an excellent, well-organized, high performing individual?" Or would they say something else?

Look at your workspace or desk, your briefcase or car. Ask, "What kind of a person works in an environment or situation like that?" Would an objective third party observer look at your work space and say you are a "highly efficient, productive, and well-organized person?" Or would they say something else?

An Outside Evaluation

Here's another exercise. Imagine an outside firm of consultants was to interview all of your co-workers and ask them this question: "What words would you use to describe that person?"

What words do people use to describe you in your absence? Based on their experience with you, with your character, and your work habits, how do people talk about you to others when you are not there? How would you like them to talk about you? What words would you like them to use? What words would help your career if used when your co-workers described you to others?

Finally, how could you develop the habits of walking, talking, dressing, working, and behaving in such a way that others describe you in the most positive and flattering way. Would it be helpful to you if people were to say, "He/she is extremely competent, efficient, honest, friendly, helpful, and gets things done quickly and well?"

How could you change or restructure your appearance and work habits so that, sometime in the future, these are the words people use when they think and talk about you? What steps could you take immediately to begin creating these words in people's minds?

BE A GOOD TEAM PLAYER

One of the most important habits you can develop in the course of your career is the habit of working well with other people. Your ability to be a good team player early in your career, and a good team leader later in your career, will do as much to increase your value to your company as any other habit or skill you can develop.

In times of economic turbulence and large-scale layoffs, researchers have found that the last people to be let go from any organization are the most popular and helpful people. The people who are kept on the longest, irrespective of economic conditions, are always the ones who are liked the most and who get along with the greatest number of people. Your job is to be one of those people.

Sometimes I ask my audience members, "How many people here work in customer service?" Very few hands go up. I then go on to point out, "Everyone is in the business of customer service. Everyone is in the business of serving customers, no matter what you do in your organization."

FOCUS ON CUSTOMER SERVICE

Develop the habit of seeing everyone around you as a customer of some kind and simultaneously seeing yourself as a customer service specialist. A customer can be defined as "Anyone you depend upon for your success at work, and anyone who depends upon you for their success at work, or in the outside world."

By this definition, you have several different customers. First, there are your external customers. These are the people who buy and use the product or service your company produces. Satisfying these people is absolutely indispensable to your success. Those people who are the most vital to serving customers of the company are always the most valuable and appreciated.

You also have another set of customers within your organization. These customers are your boss, your co-workers, and your subordinates. You depend upon each of these people for your success, and to a certain degree, each of them depends upon you. The more and better you serve your internal customers, the more productive and valuable you will be to your company.

Your Best Customer

Begin with your boss. He or she is your most important customer. You can fail to satisfy every other customer in your organization, but as long as your boss continues to like and support you, your job will be safe. On the other hand, you can please every other person inside and outside of your organization, but if you do not satisfy your boss, your job will be in jeopardy. Your boss is therefore your number one customer.

Here is an exercise. Draw up a list of everything you feel you were hired to do. Take this list to your boss and ask your boss to organize this list on the basis of his or her priorities. Ask him or her to choose your number one, most important output responsibility. Then have him choose your second most important task and so on.

Very few people do this with their bosses. The first time you approach your boss with this exercise, he or she will be both flattered and somewhat amused. But if you persist in working through this list of tasks and organization of priorities with your boss, you will both emerge from the meeting with a much better understanding of your true priorities at work.

From them on, develop the habit of always working on your boss's number one task. If your boss asks you to do a new job, immediately ask what order of priority the new task has in comparison with the other work you are doing. Make it clear that your primary aim is to work on what your boss considers to be the most important and valuable use of your time.

Help Others to Be Effective

If you have a staff of your own, perform the same exercise with them. Have each of them draw up a list answering the question, "Why am I on the payroll?" Go over these descriptions with each of your staff members and help them organize their lists by priority. From then on, do everything possible to assure that each of your staff members is working on what you consider to be the most important thing they can be doing to make the most valuable contribution possible to your organization.

Your co-workers are also your customers, because you depend upon them for certain things. You should always be looking for ways to help them do their jobs more effectively. By the Law of Reciprocity, which says that people always strive to reciprocate for anything you do for them, they will then look for ways to help you do your job even better.

In the book, *Power and Influence Beyond Formal Authority*, by John Kotter (Free Press, 1985), the author concluded that power in an organization was based on what he called, "managed dependencies." This referred to people you could influence but had no control over. They were not dependent upon you for their jobs or their incomes. These were people who were independent of you but whose help and cooperation you required if you wanted to be successful in your position.

Make up a list of all the people inside and outside of your organization whose assistance, help, cooperation, and support you need in order to do your job the very best possible. You should then make a habit of cultivating these people and looking for ways to help them to be more successful in fulfilling their responsibilities as well.

SOWING AND REAPING

In Chapter 1, I said that the Law of Cause and Effect is the granddaddy law of Western philosophy, the iron law of the cosmos. The biblical version of this law is the Law of Sowing and Reaping. This law says, "Whatsoever you sow, that also shall you reap." In the world of work, this means that, whatever you put in, or do for others, will eventually come back to you. Note that the Law of Sowing and Reaping has a specific order. First, you sow. Then, you reap. Many people try to reap before they sow or without sowing at all. But this is not the way the world works.

First, you look for ways to help other people. Then, almost automatically, people will be predisposed to helping you when the time arises. One of the great rules for success is this: "The more you give of yourself without expectation of return, the more that will come back to you from the most unexpected sources."

Develop the habit of looking for ways to put in more than you get out, to sow more than you reap, to go the extra mile, and to always do more than you are paid to do. If you always do more than you are currently being paid to do, you will be setting yourself up to be paid more in the future. Look for ways to add value continually.

President of Your Own Company

One of the most important habits you can develop to succeed in your company is the habit of viewing yourself as self-employed. See yourself as the "president" of your own personal services corporation. Act as if you own 100 percent of the shares of the company you work for. Treat the company like it belongs to you, in every respect. By developing the habit of seeing yourself as self-employed, you take complete responsibility for yourself, your company, and your career. By taking complete responsibility, and seeing yourself as the president of your own business, you change your personality and your character. Your attitude improves, and your actions become more focused, efficient, and deliberate.

A study done in New York some years ago discovered that only 3 percent of employees see themselves as self-employed. These 3 percent always seem to be paid more and promoted faster. They are the ones who take personal responsibility and personal initiative. They are action oriented in looking for ways to contribute more value to their companies. They seek out additional training experiences to increase the quality and quantity of results they can get in their jobs.

When you view yourself as the president of your own company, as completely self-responsible for your own job and your own results, you quickly come to the attention of the people who can help you the most. Doors of opportunity will open up for you. You will be promoted to positions of higher responsibility and authority. You will be more respected and esteemed by the important people around you. You will eventually leave everyone else behind.

Be Positive and Cheerful

Perhaps the most helpful decision you can make is to develop the habit of being a pleasant, positive person. Refuse to criticize, condemn, or complain. Do not engage in gossip or gripe sessions with your co-workers. Imagine that everything you say at work will be repeated and published on the company bulletin board. Guard your tongue. Instead, look for something good to say about everyone.

Always be cheerful and friendly. Be patient and easy going. Be polite and courteous. Be thoughtful and considerate. Be the kind of person everyone likes to have working for them, or likes to work for or with.

In our modern business world, it is always the people who are competent, capable, likable, and pleasant who are paid the most and promoted the fastest. Make it a habit to look for the good in every person and situation, to keep focused on helping other people, and to add value to your company. These habits will help you as much or more than anything else you could possibly do.

Action Exercises

$ Determine what you find easy to learn and easy to do and what you most enjoy doing at work; find a job doing more of that.

$ Identify your unique talents and abilities and dedicate yourself to becoming absolutely excellent in those areas.

$ Develop the habit of continually asking for, and accepting, more responsibility for results. Then move quickly when you get an opportunity to perform.

$ Work all the time you work; when you start earlier, work harder, and stay later, you quickly separate yourself from all the others.

Action Exercises, continued

$ Focus on satisfying your customers at work, both inside and outside of the company.

$ Develop the habit of working well with others; always be looking for ways to contribute, to help others to do their jobs better and faster.

$ Get the job done fast! The faster you move, the more energy you have, the more you get done, and the faster you will be paid more and promoted to higher levels of responsibility.

Work is an extension of personality. It is achievement.
It is one of the ways in which a person defines
himself, measures his worth and his humanity.

—Peter Drucker

7

The Habits of Top Businesspeople

> Continuous, unflagging effort, persistence and
> determination will win. Let not the man
> be discouraged who has these.
>
> —JAMES WHITCOMB RILEY

*E*VERYTHING THAT HAPPENS IN LIFE IS a matter of probabilities. There is a probability that virtually anything will happen. There is a probability that you will live a long, happy, healthy, and prosperous life. There is a probability that you will drive safely to and from work tomorrow. Actuaries and statisticians can determine these probabilities with considerable accuracy. The entire world of insurance, as well as much of the world of finance and investments, is based on these numbers.

Most self-made millionaires in America are entrepreneurs, business executives, or self-employed professionals. By becoming knowledgeable, proficient, and skilled in the operations of successful business, you dramatically increase the probability that you will earn a lot of money, achieve financial independence, and become a millionaire yourself in the years ahead. As it happens, all business skills and behaviors are learnable through study and practice. In this chapter, you will learn the most important habits practiced by the most successful businesspeople in every area. Your job is to adopt these habits and then apply them in all your business activities.

THE PURPOSE OF A BUSINESS

What is the purpose of a business? Some people say that it is to "make a profit." However, Peter Drucker says, "The purpose of a business is to create and keep a customer." All profits are a result of creating and keeping a sufficient number of customers and serving them in a profitable manner.

The most important habit you can develop for business success is the habit of thinking about your customers all the time. Develop an intense customer focus. Put yourself inside their hearts and minds and see everything you do from the customer's point of view. Morning, noon, and night, you must develop the habit of placing your customers in the center of your thinking in all of your business activities.

The aim of all business activities is customer satisfaction. Businesses succeed and grow because they satisfy their customers better than their competitors do. Businesses shrink and decline because they fail to supply their customers with the products and services they want at prices they are willing to pay. To be sure that you are doing the right things, one of the most important questions you ever ask is, "What does my customer consider value?"

The Power of Clarity

Perhaps the most important word in business and personal success is the word "clarity." You must be absolutely clear about who you are as a person and what you are trying to do or accomplish in your business or work. You must develop the habit of thinking carefully about every detail of your business life and then take the time to achieve absolute clarity in several different areas.

Begin with your *vision*. What is your vision for your ideal business future? If you could wave a magic wand and make your business perfect in every way, what would it look like?

In the book of Proverbs in the Bible, it says, "Where there is no vision, the people perish." In business terms, this means that where there is no clear, positive, uplifting vision for the business, people eventually lose their enthusiasm and commitment and simply go through the motions of operating the business day by day.

Just as you need an uplifting and inspiring vision for yourself and your life, you need a vision for your business. Make it a habit to continually define and clarity this picture. Practice "idealization" in the creation of this vision. Imagine that you have no limitations and that you can create your business any way you want.

Think about the Words

Think about the words you would use to describe your business if it were perfect in every respect. What would they be? What words would you want your customers to use in describing your business to other potential customers? If you could select the ideal words and put them into the mouths of your customers, what words would you choose? What words do you want the people inside and outside of your business to use to describe you and your business activities?

For example, if everyone around you described your business with the words "excellence, quality, wonderful customer service, high integrity, great people, best products, speedy follow-up, etc.," would this be helpful to you? If so, how could you organize your business activities to assure that these *are* the words people use when they think and talk about you sometime in the future. The greater clarity you have with regard to this ideal description, the easier it is for you to do the things necessary to make these words a reality.

A MISSION AND A MEASURE

What is your *mission* for your business? A mission is always defined in terms of what you want to accomplish with your business for your customers. A mission always contains a measure of some kind that you can use to determine whether or not your mission has been completed.

For example, for many years, the mission of AT&T was to "bring telephone service within the reach of every American." It took almost 100 years for AT&T to complete this mission, but the mission never changed until it was achieved.

A company might say, "Our mission is to supply our customers with the best products, backed by the best customer service in our market, and as a result, achieve sales and profit growth of 15 percent per year."

With a mission like this, strategic planning, marketing and sales, policies, and procedures all have a central focus that make it much more likely that this mission will be accomplished. What is your mission for your business and your customers?

WHY YOU DO WHAT YOU DO

What is your *purpose* for your business? The definition of purpose answers the question of "why" you are in business in the first place. What is it that you passionately want to achieve for your customers? What results do you want to get? In what ways is your business organized to improve the life of your customers in some way? Why are you doing what you are doing in the first place? The greater clarity you have with regard to your purpose, the better organized and the more efficient your entire business will be.

SET CLEAR GOALS AND OBJECTIVES

Once you are clear about your vision, mission, and purpose, you define them in terms of specific, measurable, time-bounded business goals. Your goals are the short-term, medium-term, and long-term objectives you need to reach for your business to be successful.

You need goals for how much you intend to sell and for how much you intend to earn on those sales. You need goals for the development and introduction of new products and services and the improvement of existing ones. You need goals for the types of people you want to attract and hire. You need goals for the markets you intend to enter and the amounts you intend to sell in those markets. Developing the habit of clarity about your goals gives each person in your business, and yourself, specific targets to aim at every single day.

Fortunately, in business, all goals and objectives can be expressed in financial terms. Whatever you do in your business, you can create or determine a specific financial target that will tell you whether or not you are successful. Develop the habit of thinking in financial terms and thinking in terms of net profits at every stage of your business. The most successful businesspeople think this way most of the time.

FOCUS ON MARKETING AND SALES

Every business is essentially a marketing organization. Drucker says the role of the manager is to innovate and market because these are the only two activities that create and keep customers, and ultimately, generate financial results. Surprisingly enough, most managers spend much of their time on activities that do not involve innovation or marketing.

One study asked business managers, "How important is the marketing function to your company?" Most executives replied, "very important." They then analyzed the time usage of these managers and found that only 11 percent of the working week was actually devoted to marketing. Everything else was taken up in paperwork, meetings, administration, and nonmarketing activities.

It is important for you to develop the habit of thinking about marketing and sales results most of the time. Think about your customers most of the time. Think about the things you could do, every single day, to make your products and services more attractive to more customers.

When I consult with companies on their marketing, I encourage them to establish a basic mission for their sales activities. One of the best overall missions is this: "Our mission is to get our customers to buy from us rather than from our competitors, to buy again because they are highly satisfied with their initial purchase, and then to tell and bring their friends to buy from us as well."

THE CUSTOMER IS KING

Today in our society, the customer is king—or queen. The customer decides our success or failure. The customer determines our level of growth or decline. Satisfying our customer must be the central focus and habitual way of thinking of every person in the organization. Sam Walton, founder of Wal-Mart, once said, "We all have one boss, the customer. And she can fire us any time she wants by simply deciding to shop somewhere else."

Customers buy just one thing: improvement. The reason a customer buys from you is to improve his or her life or work in some way. Your job as a businessperson is to convince your prospect that he or she will be better off buying your product or service from you, than he or she would be buying it from anyone else. Marketing, sales, and business strategy is as simple and as straightforward as that.

The customer is always right. If the customer does not buy from you, or even worse, buys from your competitor, it is because—in the customer's perception—your offerings are not attractive enough to induce the buying decision. For this reason, you must develop the "outside in" habit of dealing with your customers. You must continually look at your products, services, and what you offer from the outside. You must see yourself through the eyes of your customers so you can make whatever changes are necessary to cause your customer to prefer buying from you.

What Customers Want

Customers are incredibly selfish. They want the very most for the very least. They want the highest possible quality at the lowest possible price. They want everything to be better, faster, cheaper, and easier to purchase and use. And whatever satisfied them yesterday is not enough to satisfy them today.

To please the demanding customer of today and tomorrow, you must develop the habit of continually improving what you sell. You must be continually raising the bar on yourself. You must continually be seeking ways to provide your products better, faster, and cheaper if you want to stay ahead of your competition.

The most successful entrepreneurs develop the habit of intense market and customer orientation. They focus single-mindedly on their customers and think continually, day and night, about different ways they could please and satisfy them even more than before. Whether you start your own business or work for another business, your intense focus on your customers will do more to assure your success than any other habit you can develop in business.

THINK LIKE AN ENTREPRENEUR

Develop the habit of thinking like an entrepreneur. An entrepreneur is like a guerilla fighter in the world of capitalism. The entrepreneur has several qualities that enable him or her to start and grow a successful business against entrenched competition. Perhaps the two most important habits you can develop in entrepreneurial thinking are those of speed and flexibility.

Develop the habit of moving quickly on opportunities or problems and of doing things quickly to satisfy your customers. Large companies tend to move slowly, but entrepreneurs have the advantage of speed. Today in our society, time is a critical element of decision making in buying any product or service. The faster you can serve your customers, the more valuable and attractive they will consider you to be. Develop the habit of moving fast in selling and serving customers, and you will gain an edge in any market.

In addition, entrepreneurial thinking requires the habit of flexibility. Try. Try again. Then be willing to try something else. Remember that most things that you try in business will not succeed the first time, or even the second or third time. But the Law of Probabilities reigns supreme. The more different things you try, and the faster you try them, the more likely it is that you will discover the right method or process to make the sales and achieve the goals that you set for yourself. Keep asking, "If I was not doing this in this way, knowing what I now know, would I start it up again?" If the answer is "no," be prepared to change quickly and try something else.

Most entrepreneurial businesses eventually succeed by doing something different from what they first started. They succeed by offering different products and services to different customers than they initially planned when the business began. One of the marks of successful businesspeople is that they remain open to new ideas. They accept feedback and make quick course corrections when they find something is not working as they had expected.

SEVEN HABITS FOR BUSINESS SUCCESS

You must develop seven key habits for business success. The absence of any one of these habits can be costly—if not fatal—to your business. When you become competent and capable in each of these areas, you will be able to accomplish extraordinary results, far faster and easier than your competitors.

Plan Thoroughly

The first requirement for business success is the habit of planning. The better, more thoroughly, and more detailed that you plan your activities in advance, the faster and easier it will be for you to carry out your plans and get the results you desire once you start to work.

There is a "Six P" acronym that says, "*Proper Prior Planning Prevents Poor Performance.*" Very often, the first 20 percent of the time that you spend developing complete plans will save you 80 percent of the time later in achieving the business goals you have set.

To plan better, develop the habit of asking and answering the following questions:

- What exactly is my product or service?
- Who exactly is my customer?
- Why does my customer buy?
- What does my customer consider value?

- What is it that makes my product or service superior to that of any of my competitors?
- Why is it that my prospective customer does not buy?
- Why does my prospective customer buy from my competitor?
- What value does he/she perceive in buying from my competitor?
- How can I offset that perception and get my competitor's customers to buy from me?
- What one thing must my customer be convinced of to buy from me, rather than from someone else?

Once you have asked and answered these questions, the next stage of planning is for you to set specific targets for sales and profitability. You must determine the exact people, money, advertising, marketing, distribution, administration and service people, and facilities you will require in order to achieve your goals. The more thoroughly you plan each stage of your business activities before you begin, the greater will be the probability that you will succeed when you commence operations.

Get Organized before You Get Started

Once you have developed a complete plan for your business, you must then develop the habit of organizing the people and resources you need before you begin. In organizing, you bring together all the resources you have determined you will require in the planning process. In the military, there is a saying, "amateurs talk strategy, but professionals talk logistics." It is absolutely essential that you determine every ingredient you will need before you begin business operations and bring them together so they are ready to go when you open your doors or begin your project. The failure to provide even one important ingredient in advance can lead to the failure of the entire enterprise.

Find the Right People

The third habit you must develop is the habit of hiring the right people to help you to achieve your goals. Fully 95 percent of your success as an entrepreneur or executive will be determined by the quality of the people you recruit to work with you or to work on your team. The fact is that the best companies have the best people. The second best companies have the second best people. The third best companies have the average or mediocre people, and they are on their way out of business.

Delegate Wisely

The fourth habit you need to develop for business success is the habit of proper delegation. You must develop the ability to delegate the right task, to the right person, in the right way. The inability to delegate effectively can be the cause of failure or underperformance of the individual and can even bring about failure of the business.

When people start in business, they usually do everything themselves. As they grow and expand, the job becomes too large for one person, so they hire someone to do part of it. However, if they are not careful, they try to retain control of the task and never fully hand over both authority and responsibility to the other person.

In our Advanced Coaching and Mentoring Programs (see Appendix), we teach executives and entrepreneurs to identify the two or three things they do that contribute the most value to their companies and then delegate the rest. You must do the same thing. You must learn to think in terms of "getting things done through others" rather than trying to do them yourself. It is the only way you can leverage and multiply your special skills and abilities.

Inspect What You Expect

The fifth requirement for business success is for you to develop the habit of proper supervision. You must set up a system to monitor the task and make sure it is being done as agreed upon. The rule is, "inspect what you expect." Once you have delegated a task to the right person in the right way, it is essential that you monitor the performance of the task and make sure it is done on schedule and to the required level of quality. Remember, delegation is not abdication. You are still responsible for the ultimate results of the delegated tasks. You must stay on top of it.

When you have delegated a task, set up a system of reporting so that you are always informed as to the status of the work. Be sure that the other person knows what is to be done, and when, and to what standard. Your job is then to make sure that he or she has the time and resources necessary to get the job done satisfactorily. The more important the job, the more often you should check on progress.

Measure What Gets Done

The sixth practice of successful entrepreneurs and executives is the habit of measuring performance. You must set specific, measurable standards and score cards for the results that you require. You have to set specific timelines and deadlines to make sure you "make your numbers" on schedule. Everyone who is expected to carry out a task must know with complete clarity the targets that he or she is aiming at, how successful performance will be measured, and when the expected results are due.

In our Focal Point process, we teach the importance of your selecting and defining specific goals, measures and activities that are then used as benchmarks for performance. Jim Collins, in his book *From Good to Great* (HarperCollins, 2001), refers to the importance of selecting the "economic denominator" for a company, and for individual goals and objectives within that company. Whichever number you choose, it must be clear to everyone, and it must be monitored continually to make sure everyone is on track.

Keep People Informed

The seventh habit for businesspeople is the habit of reporting results regularly and accurately. People around you need to know what is going on. Your bankers need to know your financial results. Your staff needs to know the status and the situation of your company. Your key people, at all levels, need to know what results are being achieved.

In a study on workplace motivation, several thousand employees said the most important factor leading to job satisfaction was, "being in the know." People in an organization have a deep need to know and understand what is going on around them in relation to their work. The more thoroughly and accurately you report to people the details and situation of your business, the happier they will be and the better results they will get.

THE HABITS OF WINNERS IN BUSINESS

To succeed greatly in business, and to become a self-made millionaire, you need to develop additional habits as well. One of these habits is the determination to win, to succeed, to outperform your competition, and to ultimately be successful. This competitive instinct and determination to win in the face of any obstacle or difficulty is a chief motivating power that drives entrepreneurs and eventually assures successful careers.

The determination to succeed is an absolutely essential habit for you to develop, through practice, by never considering the possibility of failure. Instead, you use speed and flexibility to find solutions to problems, to overcome obstacles, and to achieve business goals, no matter what is happening around you. This decision, or attitude toward winning, motivates and enthuses other people and enables ordinary people to achieve extraordinary results.

Be Open to New Information

Develop the habit of questioning your assumptions on a regular basis, especially when you experience resistance or temporary failure. Many people leap to conclusions and assume things about their customers, their competitors, and their markets that have no basis in fact at all. Always be prepared to ask yourself, "What do I base this assumption on? What are my facts? What evidence do I have? What is my proof?" And most important, be prepared to ask, "What if my assumptions about this customer, product, service, market or competitor were not true at all? What changes would I have to make?"

The most dangerous assumption an entrepreneur or businessperson can make is that a large enough and profitable enough market exists for a particular product or service. Very often this is not the case at all. The primary reason for the dotcom implosion was because there was no real market for the products and services the dotcom companies were offering. They fell into a false form of thinking called "argument by assertion." People often get caught up in an argument because it is asserted loudly and vigorously, even though it may have no substance at all. Assertion is not proof.

Abraham Lincoln was once trying to make a point to the members of his cabinet. He asked this question, "If you took a dog, and called the dog's tail a leg, how many legs would the dog now have?"

Several members of his cabinet suggested the answer "Five."

At this, Lincoln pointed out, "No, the dog still has only four legs. Calling a tail a leg does not make it a leg."

The moral of this story is that asserting, wishing, or hoping that a fact is true does not have any bearing on the ultimate truth of the statement. Only facts are facts. It is essential that you develop the habit of sorting out facts from fantasy and making your decisions based on demonstrable, provable truths with regard to customers, markets, products, and services.

Think before Acting

In a fast changing business world, an important habit you can develop is the habit of thinking before acting. Often, when we are pressured from all sides with decisions that have to be made, we leap to conclusions and make decisions without carefully considering all the possible ramifications of those decisions. Instead, develop the habit of buying time between the pressure to make a decision and the actual decision itself. There is a rule that says, "If the decision does not have to be made now, it has to not be made now."

Your mind is incredibly powerful, and never more so than when you give it time to reflect before you make a decision. Make it a habit of asking for a day, or a weekend, or even a week or a month, before you make a final decision. Put it off as long as possible. The very act of allowing the various pieces of information to settle in your brain will enable you to make a much better decision than you might have made if you decided too quickly.

It is amazing how many people say, "If I had just thought about that for a little while, I would have made a completely different decision." This is almost always the case. Make it a habit to delay and defer decisions as long as you possibly can. They will invariably be better decisions when you finally come around to making them.

Build a Mastermind Network

Another habit for business success is the habit of masterminding with other people, both inside and outside your company. In our Advanced Coaching and Mentoring Program in San Diego, we work with successful entrepreneurs to create masterminding groups with other entrepreneurs to develop business ideas and make better business decisions. The result is absolutely astonishing! Very often, entrepreneurs who have been struggling with business questions and problems for many months get solutions from the members of their mastermind group in a matter of minutes.

A mastermind group can be either structured or unstructured. Either one will be effective. In a structured mastermind group, a particular question such as "How can we increase sales in this market?" is thrown out, and everyone brainstorms different ideas that they have found or are trying in their own businesses. Very often, an idea that has proven successful in one type of business is exactly the idea that works successfully for a completely different business.

In an unstructured brainstorming session, people get together and "free-flow." They talk in general terms about business, the economy, sales, customers, competitors, and so on. Out of this ferment often come great ideas that members of the mastermind group can use in their own activities.

If you own your own business, you should sit down with your key people and mastermind a couple of times each week. Talk about how the business is going and some of the problems you are facing. Ask if anyone has any suggestions or ideas. Listen attentively without interrupting when people make suggestions. Go around the table and invite input from everyone. You will be absolutely amazed at the quality of ideas that seem to emerge when you practice masterminding and brainstorming on a regular basis.

THE FOUNDATIONS OF BUSINESS SUCCESS

There are seven key result areas in management. All business success is a result of working regularly in these seven areas to achieve better results. These are all habitual ways of thinking for business success and profitability.

Productivity

The first key result area—or habit—that you need to develop is the habit of thinking continually in terms of increasing productivity. The goal of strategic planning is to "increase return on equity." It is to increase the financial results and outputs relative to the costs and inputs involved. It is to get more sales, revenues, and profits out of the business than are currently being achieved.

All successful businesspeople think continually in terms of increasing productivity. They look for ways to do more with less, to get more out at a lower cost. Even in times of economic growth and prosperity, they are continually looking for ways to increase results at lower costs.

Look at what you are doing today. How could you increase the productivity, performance, and output of yourself and your business by changing the things you do? What could you do more of, or less of? What could you start doing that you are not doing today? What could you stop doing altogether? What is it that you are doing today that, knowing what you now know, you wouldn't start again today? The answers to these questions can lead you to productivity breakthroughs that will dramatically improve your financial results.

Customer Satisfaction

The second key result area, which we have already discussed, is the habit of thinking in terms of customer satisfaction all the time. The starting point of developing this habit is for you to be absolutely clear about how your customers define satisfaction. What has to happen for your customers to be so happy with you that they buy again and tell their friends?

Domino's Pizza is famous for having defined customer satisfaction as "speed." Thomas Monahan, the founder of Domino's Pizza, found that when people ordered a pizza, they were already hungry. For them, the speed at which the pizza was delivered was more important than the relative quality of the food. With this single insight, Monahan built a 7,000-unit pizza empire that extends around the world and retired with a personal fortune of $1.8 billion dollars. Not a bad return on a single insight into what customers really wanted! How do your customers define satisfaction?

Profitability

The third habit you need to develop is the habit of thinking in terms of profitability all the time. Many businesses focus too much on the top line, on gross sales, rather than on the bottom line, on net profits. As Baron de Rothschild, in his Maxims For Success said, "Always concentrate on net profits."

You should analyze each of your products, services, customers, and markets to determine exactly how profitable they are. Many companies today find that their largest customers, because of high servicing costs and discounts, are not particularly profitable at all. Many companies are finding that certain products and services they sell in large volume are not profitable because many hidden costs are involved. The companies find they are actually breaking even, or even losing money, on their best-selling products or services.

What are your most profitable products? What are your most profitable services? Who are your most profitable customers? What are your most profitable markets? What products, services, customers, or markets should you emphasize or de-emphasize? Always think in terms of the bottom line, of the dollar-for-dollar profitability of each one of your business activities.

Quality

The fourth key result area is the habit of thinking in terms of quality all the time. Customers only buy a product or service because they feel it is of higher quality in some way than that of competitive offerings. How do your customers define quality? What qualities or attributes of what you sell cause them to buy from you in the first place? What quality elements do they see in your competitors? How could you offset these elements to get them to buy from you?

One of your most important activities should be regular customer interaction, asking your customers why they buy from you and how you could improve your quality and service to them. Practice the CANEI method or "Continuous And Never Ending Improvement." Remember, whatever got you to where you are today is not enough to keep you there.

Whatever you are doing today, and however well you are doing it, you will have to do it considerably better a year from now if you still want to be in business.

The most important goal you can set for yourself and your business is to "be the best" in some area that is important to your customers. This is not only the key to increased sales and profitability but also the key to motivation and commitment among the people who work for the company. Everyone likes to be part of an organization that is committed to winning, to excellence, to serving customers better than anyone else.

Employees

The fifth key result area in business is the habit of thinking in terms of people building. In business today, your primary assets walk out the door at 5:00 P.M. Of all assets, only people can be made to appreciate in value when time and training are invested in them. Your people are everything. All productivity comes from them; there is no other source. All profitability comes from your people. All sales and fulfillment come from your people. Your ability to select them and then to motivate and inspire them is essential for your success.

Develop the habit of spending time with the most important people in your business. Ask them for their opinions. Compliment on them on their accomplishments. Take them out for coffee or lunch. Make them feel important and valuable. Remember, the very best companies have the very best people. And these people are invariably the ones who are the happiest because of the way they are treated by others, especially by their bosses.

Organizational Development

The sixth habit you can develop to build your business is the habit of organizational development. This habit requires that you continually look for ways to organize and reorganize your business so that it functions more efficiently and effectively. You continually move people around to assure the job gets done better, faster, and with less friction or interruption.

Some years ago, if a company announced that it was going through a "major reorganization," it would be a sign that there were serious problems in that company. Today, however, with the rate of rapid change in the business world around you, you and your company should be in a state of continuous reorganization. Every day, week, and month, you should be thinking about how you can deploy and redeploy people and resources to assure the highest level of productivity, performance, and output.

Within the context of organizational development, you should develop the habit of not only learning and growing continuously yourself, but also thinking in terms of training and learning experiences for the key members of your staff. Sometimes, one additional skill is all a person needs to dramatically improve his or her productivity and contribution to the organization.

You should not only offer learning opportunities to your staff but also offer to pay for any courses or seminars that they take to improve their business ability. Encourage them to be self-directed learners. Encourage them to attend courses and seminars offered in your community that will help them to improve their performance and get better results. This is one of the most powerful motivational techniques of all.

Innovation

The seventh habit you can develop is the habit of continuous innovation. As we discussed earlier in this chapter, you should encourage everyone to be thinking creatively all the time.

One way to encourage creativity is to ask each employee to bring an idea to each weekly staff meeting. Start off the meeting by going around the table and having everyone contribute their ideas. Lead the general discussion about these ideas. When someone comes up with a great idea, lead the group in applause. Thank and congratulate the person. Encourage them to keep thinking in this way throughout the week.

You should have a company suggestion box. Offer a financial prize each week for the best idea to increase sales or cut costs. It doesn't have to be very large, $5 or $10, to motivate people to think creatively all the time.

Announce the award for the best idea at the weekly staff meeting. Hand it out and congratulate the person. Shake his or her hand. Lead a round of applause. You will be absolutely amazed at how many good ideas your people will come up with when they are encouraged and rewarded for thinking creatively.

The most important area for continuous innovation is to your products and services. Remember, fully 80 percent of products and services being sold today will be obsolete within five years. You must be developing and producing product and service innovations as a regular part of your business activities. If you don't, your competitors will. One major innovation by a determined competitor can put you out of business. Be a leader, not a follower.

Think ahead and look at different ways you can organize and reorganize your business to do things better, faster, and cheaper than your competitors. Think of new products and services you can offer. Think of new markets you can enter. Think of different ways you can offset advantages enjoyed by your competitors. Think of different ways you could dominate your markets. The more you dedicate yourself to generating ideas, the more and better ideas you will come up with.

BRAINPOWER IS THE MOST IMPORTANT
COMPETITIVE ADVANTAGE

As you read through the suggestions in this chapter for the development of business habits, you will probably notice that none of them cost any money. Every single one of these habits of thinking is learnable, via practice and repetition. You can develop them by simply reflecting upon the idea or habit on a regular basis.

The more you think about the importance of planning, the more habitual it will become for you to plan thoroughly in advance. The more you think about the importance of hiring and staffing, the more habitual it will become for you to think through the decision carefully before you hire a new person.

The more you think about customer satisfaction, the more it will become a habit for you to think in terms of different ways you can satisfy your customers better than anyone else. The Law of Concentration says, "Whatever you dwell upon grows and expands in your life." The more you think about any one of these habits or behaviors, the more you incorporate that habit or behavior into your personality. Eventually, it becomes a permanent part of the way you think, walk, talk, act, and get results.

NO ONE IS BETTER OR SMARTER

Remember, no one is smarter than you, and no one is better than you. If someone is doing better than you are today, it is because they have developed a particular habit of thinking and acting before you have. And whatever other people have learned, you can learn as well.

The very fact that there are many hundreds of thousands of men and women who have started from nothing and become millionaires in business and entrepreneurship means you can achieve these goals for yourself, if you just learn how. The only limits on your results are the limits you place on yourself with your own thinking. By developing the thinking habits of successful entrepreneurs and businesspeople, you will eventually overcome all of your obstacles and difficulties, achieve all your financial goals, and become financially independent. Nothing can stop you.

Action Exercises

$ Determine the most important thing you could do immediately to increase the probabilities that you successfully achieve your most important business goal. Then take action on it immediately.

$ Create an ideal future vision for your business and your career. If your situation were perfect three to five years from now, what would it look like?

$ What is the most important difference or improvement you make in the life and work of your customers, and how could you do this in an excellent fashion?

Action Exercises, continued

$ What is your greatest personal strength in your business, and how could you organize your time so that you are doing more of it?

$ What is your biggest weakness in your business, and how could you develop yourself in this area, or compensate for it?

$ What innovations could you make in your products or services that would make them more attractive to your customers of today and tomorrow?

$ What are your most profitable products, services, markets, customers, and activities, and what steps could you take immediately to focus more of your resources in those areas?

Nothing contributes so much to the happiness
and prosperity of a country as high profits.

—DAVID RICARDO

The Habits for Marketing and Sales Success

> All business success rests on something labeled
> a sale, which at least momentarily weds
> company and customer.
>
> —THOMAS J. PETERS & ROBERT H. WATERMAN, JR.

*C*ALVIN COOLIDGE ONCE SAID, "THE business of America is business." Coolidge, the 30th President of the United States, also said, "No enterprise can exist for itself alone. It ministers to some great need, it performs some great service, not for itself, but for others; or failing therein, it ceases to be profitable and ceases to exist."

America is the greatest commercial society in history. Virtually all wealth is based on somebody producing a product or service and selling it to someone else at a profit. America is considered the most entrepreneurial country in the world according to the Organization for Economic Cooperation and Development (OECD 2003). It is more open to more people who want to create and sell products and services to others, and the market is larger than in any other country or geographical entity.

Revenues and profits from sales pay all wages, all taxes, all education, all medical expenses, and for all hospitals, schools, roads, airports, office buildings, defense, welfare, unemployment insurance, and everything else of a material nature in America. Where there are high sales, there is high prosperity. Where there are low sales, there is low prosperity, lack of economic opportunity, decline, and ultimately failure.

THE REASON FOR SUCCESS OR FAILURE

Dun & Bradstreet (D&B) offers a credit rating service that includes most of the businesses in the U.S. Every year, active businesses are invited to contribute their financial information to this database, which is then made available for credit purposes to prospective suppliers and vendors.

Over the years, many thousands of companies close down, merge, or go bankrupt. Each year, D&B conducts a study to determine the major factors leading to business failure in that particular 12-month period. Over the years, the reasons for business failure have been high interest costs, changes in technology, poor management, or under-capitalization. Often it is high inventory relative to sales or too much debt.

Not long ago, D&B took all the statistics it had generated on failing companies over the years and ran them through a supercomputer. This program sorted out all the variables and distilled business success and failure into a simple conclusion: Businesses succeed because of high sales; businesses fail because of low sales. All else is commentary.

The rule is, "Nothing happens until a sale takes place, until someone sells something to someone." Businesses succeed because they make sufficient sales and generate sufficient profitability to survive and grow in the current marketplace. Businesses fail because of declining sales and revenues, which ultimately leads to the collapse of the enterprise.

The Most Important Number

The most important single number in the operation of any business is cash flow. In the wake of the accounting scandals among major companies on Wall Street, the accounting profession has reverted to focusing on what they consider to be the most important single economic denominator of business success: free cash flow.

Free cash flow is the amount of money left over or generated by the activities of the business after all expenses have been subtracted. It is measurable, quantifiable, and definite. It exists. It is there in the bank account to be accounted for and spent by the business. It cannot be faked. It is a real number. It is the critical indicator of business success or failure.

Where does free cash flow come from? It comes from marketing and sales, less all the costs of generating those sales and fulfilling those orders. There is no other source. All mortgages, loans, advances, and lines of credit must ultimately be justified and repaid out of marketing and sales revenues.

Your Critical Determinant of Contribution

The greater influence you have on the cash flow of your enterprise, the more valuable and important you are to that business. The more you can contribute toward increasing cash flow, the higher you will be paid, and the faster you will be promoted. Sales are everything.

One of the most important habits you can develop on your way to becoming a self-made millionaire is the habit of sales orientation. All successful entrepreneurs and business people are intensely customer and sales focused. They think about their customers and how to serve them all the time. They have what Tom Peters calls, "an obsession with customer service."

They think continually about how to make more sales to more and better customers. They are fixated on getting and keeping customers, on making more and better sales, and on developing larger and more profitable markets. They think about customers and sales night and day. This is the critical habit you must develop to become a self-made millionaire as an entrepreneur or as a key person in any business.

THE FOUR HABITS OF MARKETING SUCCESS

Several strategies, or habits of thinking and acting, that you can learn through practice will make you a much more efficient and effective businessperson, especially in the area of generating sales, revenues, and cash flow for your business. These are specialization, differentiation, segmentation, and concentration. Let me describe each of them in turn.

Specialize in One Area

To develop the habit of specialization requires that you decide clearly the area in which you are going to specialize to compete and win in the current market. Individuals and organizations that specialize are far more effective in creating and keeping customers than companies that generalize or try to offer too many products and services to too many customers and markets, in too many ways, at too many price points.

You can specialize in one of three main areas: products or services, customers, or markets. You specialize in a particular product or service when you decide that you are going to focus all of your energies on producing and selling a specific product or service that achieves a specific goal for your customers. For example, if you specialize in fast food, you only produce foods that can be picked up and consumed on the premises or immediately thereafter. You do not offer any product or service that doesn't fall into the category of fast food.

If you specialize in automotive transportation, you do not manufacture tractors, photocopiers or refrigerators, even though your plants or factories could be adapted to produce these products over time. You specialize in automobiles.

Just as the pellets of a shotgun shell will spread soon after emerging from the barrel, there is a natural tendency in personal and business life toward diffusion of effort. There are so many opportunities and possibilities that the urge to generalize and offer a wide range of products and services serving a wide range of customers and markets is very tempting. But successful individuals and organizations resist the temptation to spread their efforts and, instead, dedicate themselves to specializing in a particular area where they have the ability to achieve market dominance. You must do the same.

Be Different from All the Rest

The second habit for marketing success, and perhaps the most important, is the habit of differentiating your product or service from that of all other competitors. Customers buy only what they consider to be "the best" as it relates to their specific need at the moment. Sometimes the best is speedy delivery. Sometimes it is long-term durability of a product. Sometimes it is convenience or low price. You must decide where and how you are going to differentiate yourself from your competitors.

This is called your area of competitive advantage or your area of excellence. Your area of differentiation describes what you offer to your customers that makes your product or service superior to anything else available. How clear you are with regard to your competitive advantage largely determines the effectiveness of all your sales and marketing efforts.

Without a clear competitive advantage, an area of excellence or superiority, it is impossible for you to survive and thrive in a tough market. As Jack Welch, past president of General Electric, once said, "If you don't have competitive advantage, don't compete."

Ask yourself, "What is my competitive advantage today?" What makes your product or service superior to that of any of your competitors? It may be something as simple as the location of your business. It may be something less tangible, such as the personalities of the key people who sell and deliver your product or service. Many entrepreneurial businesses are started and become successful because of the personality and character of a single individual who customers prefer to deal with rather than with anyone else in that same field.

DETERMINE YOUR COMPETITIVE ADVANTAGE

You should be able to write down your area of competitive advantage on the back of a business card. Once defined, it becomes the core message you convey in all of your advertising and sales. Everyone in your company must know with absolute clarity why and how what you offer is better in a particular way. Everyone must know why customers should buy your product or service rather than any similar product or service available. The determination of this area of excellence, the development of this competitive advantage, is the fundamental key to business success.

What is your competitive advantage today? What will your competitive advantage be three to five years from now? What should it be? What could it be? What are the trends in your business, and what will you have to be doing in an excellent fashion three to five years from now in order to survive and thrive in the marketplace of the future?

Your ability to think ahead and answer these questions, and then to take whatever steps are necessary today to be sure you have the competitive advantage sometime in the future, is essential to your long-term success.

What should you be absolutely *excellent* at doing for your customer? Looking around at your marketplace today, and at the reasons why people do not buy from you—or even worse, buy from your competitors—what competitive advantage do you need to develop if you want to lead your field?

What *could* your competitive advantage be? If you were to reorganize your business, change your product or service offerings, change your market or methods of sales, marketing, manufacturing or distribution, what could your competitive advantage be sometime in the future? What steps could you or should you take today in order to assure that your products and services are clearly superior to that of your competitors sometime in the future?

The habit of asking and answering these questions for yourself is the core responsibility of the entrepreneur or executive. Developing your competitive advantage is the key to success in any business. It is the primary reason for high sales and high profitability in any business, large or small.

Determine Your Best Potential Customers

The third habit of marketing is the habit of segmentation. Many people might be able to buy what you sell, but they are not all prospective customers for you and your business. Your ability to analyze your market and create a profile of the exact type of customer who can most benefit from the product or service you specialize in and appreciate what your product or service does better is the key to marketing success.

In any market, there is a profile of potential buyers who are "high probability customers." These are people who very much value what it is you do so well. These prospects are more willing than most prospects to buy from you. They are willing to pay you more money for your particular product or service because they value your offering more than those of your competitors. They will pay faster and more dependably than other prospects. Your ability to identify this ideal customer is the key to focusing your marketing and sales efforts and activities.

Focus and Concentrate Your Sales Efforts

The fourth habit for marketing success is the habit of concentration. Your ability to concentrate in general is essential for achieving success in any activity. The ability to concentrate in particular—and to focus all of your marketing and sales efforts and energies on those specific customers you have identified as most likely to benefit from what you sell—is the key to maximizing your sales, revenue, and profits.

Develop the habit of thinking like a marketing genius. Develop the habit of asking yourself questions such as, "In what areas do we specialize? In what areas are we superior to our competitors in our area of specialization? Who are the most desirable and attractive market segments for what it is that we do better than anyone else? How can we organize ourselves to concentrate all of our resources on selling more to those customers who most appreciate what we can do for them better than our competitors?" Your ability to ask and answer these questions accurately can transform your business results.

THE SEVEN P FORMULA

Once you have developed your marketing strategy, there is a Seven P Formula you should use to continually evaluate and reevaluate your business activities. These seven are: product, price, promotion, place, packaging, positioning, and people. As products, markets, customers, and needs change rapidly, you must continually revisit these seven Ps to make sure you are on track and achieving the maximum results possible for you in today's marketplace.

Product

To begin, develop the habit of looking at your product as though you were an outside marketing consultant having been brought in to help your company decide whether or not it is in the right business at this time. Ask critical questions such as, "Is your current product or service, or mix of products or services appropriate and suitable for the market and the customers of today?"

Whenever you are having difficulty selling as much of your products or services as you'd like, you need to develop the habit of assessing your business honestly and asking, "Are these the right products or services for our customers today?"

Is there any product or service you are offering today that, knowing what you now know, you would not bring out again today? Compared to your competitors, is your product or service superior in some significant way to anything else available? If so, what is it? If not, could you develop an area of superiority? Should you be offering this product or service at all in the current marketplace?

TAKE THE BUNDLE OF RESOURCES VIEWPOINT

Develop the habit of looking upon your business as a "bundle of resources." At one time, your business did not exist. When it began, you brought together a variety of resources, in the form of people, money, facilities, and so on, to produce a product or service to sell in the market that existed at that time.

This bundle of resources that makes up your company is very much like a pistol. It can be aimed and fired in different directions. This bundle of resources can be combined and recombined to produce new products or services as the market changes.

Resist the temptation to become rigid in your ideas about the products or services you sell. Be flexible and open to the possibility or necessity of offering something completely new or different. See your business as a bundle of resources that has the ability to offer a wide range of products or services if the market demands it.

Prices Deserve Attention

The second P in the formula has to do with price. Develop the habit of continually examining and reexamining the prices of the products and services that you sell to make sure they are still appropriate to the realities of the current market. Sometimes you need to lower your prices. At other times, it may be appropriate to raise your prices. Many companies have found that the profitability of certain products or services does not justify the amount of effort and resources that go into producing them. By raising their prices, they may lose a percentage of their customers, but the remaining percentage generates a profit on every sale. Could this be appropriate for you?

Sometimes you need to change your terms and conditions of sale. Sometimes, by spreading your price over a series of months or years, you can sell far more than you are today, and the interest that you can charge on the amount you carry will more than make up for the delay in cash receipts. Sometimes you can combine products and services together with special offers and special promotions. Sometimes you can include free additional items that cost you very little to produce but that make your prices appear far more attractive to your customers.

In business, as in nature, whenever you experience resistance or frustration in any part of your sales or marketing activities, be open to revisiting that area. Be open to the possibility that your current pricing structure is not ideal for the current market. Be open to the need to revise your prices, if necessary, to remain competitive, to survive, and thrive in a fast-changing marketplace.

Promotion

The third habit in marketing and sales is for you to develop the habit of thinking in terms of promotion all the time. Promotion includes all the ways you tell your customers about your products or services and how you then market and sell to them.

Small changes in the way you promote and sell your products can lead to dramatic changes in your results. Even small changes in your advertising can lead immediately to higher sales. Experienced copywriters can often increase the response rate from advertising by 500 percent by simply changing the headline on an advertisement.

Large and small companies in every industry continually experiment with different ways of advertising, promoting, and selling their products and services. And here is the rule: whatever method of marketing and sales you are using today will, sooner or later, stop working. Sometimes it will stop working for reasons you know, and sometimes it will be for reasons that you don't know. In either case, your methods of marketing and sales will eventually stop working, and you will have to develop new sales, marketing, and advertising approaches, offerings, and strategies.

SALES TRAINING CAN DOUBLE YOUR SALES

One of the most important parts of promoting your product or service has to do with the exact way the product is sold when your customers are face to face with your salespeople. What exact words are used? What exact offer is made? What exact process is used to identify the customer's needs, make presentations, and close the sale?

Fully 70 percent of salespeople in America have never been given this type of sales training. Instead, all they have received from their companies is "product training." Many companies are operated by people who have not been in the sales field themselves; as a result, some executives are blind to the fact that approximately 80 percent of sales success is determined by the quality of the salespeople that end up face to face with the customer. Small improvements in the quality of this interface can lead to dramatic improvements in the level of sales, no matter what the product and service, and no matter what the state of the current market.

In my personal work with more than 500 companies and more than 500,000 salespeople, I have found that small changes in sales proficiency often lead to rapid increases in sales results. I have worked with literally thousands of individuals and hundreds of companies who have been able to increase their sales five and ten times by learning and practicing better sales methodologies.

Place

The fourth P in the marketing mix is the place where your product or service is actually sold. Develop the habit of reviewing and reflecting upon the exact location where the customer meets the salesperson. Sometimes a change in place can lead to a rapid increase in sales.

You can sell your product in many different places. Some companies use direct selling, sending their salespeople out to personally meet and talk with the prospect. Some sell by telemarketing. Some sell through catalogs or mail order. Some sell at trade shows, or in retail establishments. Some sell in joint ventures with other similar products or services. Some companies use manufacturers' representatives or distributors. Many companies use a combination of one or more of these methods.

In each case, the entrepreneur must make the right choice about the very best location or place for the customer to receive essential buying information on the product or service needed to make a buying decision. What is yours? In what way should you change it? Where else could you offer your products or services?

Packaging

The fifth element in the marketing mix is the packaging. Develop the habit of standing back and looking at every visual element in the packaging of your product or service through the eyes of a critical prospect. Remember, people form their first impression about you within the first 30 seconds of seeing you or some element of your company. Small improvements in the packaging or external appearance of your product or service can often lead to completely different reactions from your customers.

With regard to the packaging of your company, your product, or service, you should think in terms of everything that the customer sees from the first moment of contact with your company all the way through the purchasing process.

Packaging refers to the way your product or service appears from the outside. Packaging also refers to your people and how they dress and groom. It refers to your offices, your waiting rooms, your brochures, your correspondence, and every single visual element about your company. Everything counts. Everything helps or hurts. Everything affects your customer's confidence about dealing with you.

When IBM started under the guidance of Thomas J. Watson, Sr., he very early concluded that fully 99 percent of the visual contact a customer would have with his company, at least initially, would be represented by IBM salespeople. Because IBM was selling relatively sophisticated high-tech equipment, Watson knew customers would have to have a high level of confidence in the credibility of the salesperson. He therefore instituted a dress and grooming code that became an inflexible set of rules and regulations within IBM.

As a result, every salesperson was required to look like a professional in every respect. Every element of their clothing, including dark suits, dark ties, white shirts, conservative hairstyles, shined shoes, clean fingernails, and every other feature gave off the message of professionalism and competence. One of the highest compliments a person could receive was, "You look like someone from IBM."

REVAMP YOUR PERSONAL IMAGE

Many companies change their results by establishing a dress code for the people in their company who deal with their customers. They know the importance of appearance. During the dotcom boom of the late 90s, when business was exploding, many young dotcom executives would come to work in shorts, sandals, and undershirts. But they would keep a business suit nearby to change into if a customer or venture capitalist came to visit. They recognized that people make lasting and important decisions based on appearances.

Many of my entrepreneurial clients return home from Focal Point Coaching and Mentoring sessions and completely revamp their images, changing their ways of dressing and grooming so they look better and more credible to their customers.

They often renovate their offices, especially their waiting rooms, so that when their customers visit, the first thing they see are beautiful, professionally appointed premises. In every case, my clients report to me that their customers are more open and receptive to buying, and easier to deal with, when their surroundings are attractive and professional.

Ask yourself some questions. Do you dress and look like a first class professional, in every respect, when you go to work, and when you meet with your customers or suppliers? Are you proud of the appearance of your staff? Do you feel happy to introduce your staff, with the way they currently dress and look on the outside, to your customers and suppliers? Are your offices neat, clean, organized, and attractive? Are you proud to have critical customers visit you and walk around your facilities?

Especially, do your products look absolutely excellent on the outside? Are your brochures beautifully designed and printed? Is your packaging attractive? Are you proud of every visual element that strikes the eyes of your customers in their dealings with you? Is there anything you could or should change or improve to create a better visual image for your customers? If your answer is "yes" for any reason, you should act immediately to change what needs to be changed.

Positioning

The next P of the marketing mix is positioning. You should develop the habit of thinking continually about how you are positioned in the hearts and minds of your customers. How do people think about you and talk about you when you are not present? How do people think and talk about your company? What positioning do you have in your market, in terms of the specific words that people use when they describe you and your offerings to others?

In the famous book by Reis and Trout, *Positioning* (McGraw-Hill Trade, 2000), the authors point out that how you are seen and thought about by your customers is the critical determinant of your success in a competitive marketplace. Attribution theory says most customers think of you in terms of a single attribute, either positive or negative. Sometimes it is "service." Sometimes it is "excellence." Sometimes it is "quality engineering," as it is with Mercedes Benz. Sometimes it is "the ultimate driving machine," as it is with BMW. In every case, how deeply entrenched that attribute is in the minds of your customers and prospective customers determines how readily they will buy your product or service and how much they will pay.

Develop the habit of thinking about how you could improve your positioning. Begin by determining the position that you would like to have. If you could create an ideal impression in the hearts and minds of your customers, what would it be? What would you have to do in every customer interaction to get your customers to think and talk about you in that specific way? What changes do you need to make in the way you interact with customers today in order to be seen as the very best choice for your customers of tomorrow?

People Are Everything

The final P of the marketing mix is people. Develop the habit of thinking in terms of the people inside and outside of your business who are responsible for every element of your sales and marketing strategy and activities.

It is amazing how many entrepreneurs and businesspeople will work extremely hard to think through every element of the marketing strategy and the marketing mix and then pay little attention to the fact that every single decision and policy has to be carried out by a specific person, in a specific way. Your ability to select, recruit, hire, and retain the proper people, with the skills and abilities to do the job you need to have done, is more important than everything else put together.

In his best-selling book, *Good to Great* (HarperCollins, 2001), Jim Collins discovered that the most important factor applied by the best companies was that they first of all "got the right people on the bus, and the wrong people off the bus." Once these companies had hired the right people, the second step was to "get the right people in the right seats on the bus."

To be successful in business, you must develop the habit of thinking in terms of exactly who is going to carry out each task and responsibility. In many cases, it is not possible to move forward until you can attract and put the right person into the right position. Many of the best business plans ever developed sit on shelves today because they could not find the key people who could execute those plans.

PUTTING IT ALL TOGETHER

You have now developed the habit of marketing orientation, continually thinking in terms of marketing strategy, and the Seven P Formula.

You have developed the habit of customer orientation—continually thinking about your customers and how your activities at every level affect them and influence their buying decisions.

In your development of the habit of sales orientation, you must develop several smaller but equally important habits to maximize your business potential. Sales orientation requires you to think continually about how to make more sales, better, faster, easier, and more profitably than ever before. In reality, the sales effort is where the rubber meets the road in every competitive business.

An average product that is aggressively sold by first class professionals will dramatically outsell a superior product sold in a mediocre way by untrained salespeople. There are seven key habits you must develop as a sales expert. They are: prospecting, establishing rapport, identifying needs, presenting solutions, answering objections, closing the sale, and getting resales and referrals. They proceed in order. Habitually thinking about each of these seven elements of the sales process, and how each of them could be improved, is the key to increasing your sales, your revenues, and your profitability.

Find Ideal Customers

The first habit of top salespeople is that they think about prospecting most of the time. To succeed greatly in sales, you must develop the habit of spending more time with better prospects. You must develop the habit of prospecting and looking for new business 80 percent of the time. You must be prospecting morning, noon, and night. You must never relax in your prospecting efforts until you have so many customers that you do not have enough time left in the day to sell and satisfy all the people who want to buy from you.

If you have analyzed your business in terms of specialization, differentiation, segmentation, and concentration, you will already have a good idea of the customers and prospects you should focus on. If you have analyzed your business in terms of the seven Ps, Product, Price, Promotion, Place, Packaging, Positioning, and People, you will be able to zero in on exactly those prospects who can most benefit from the product or service you offer. But you must develop the habit of thinking about prospecting all the time, whether you are a salesperson or owner of the entire company.

Focus on Relationships

The second habit for sales success is the habit of focusing on the relationship before anything else. You should focus on establishing rapport, trust, and credibility with each prospect from the first contact. The most successful salespeople, once they have identified a key prospect, take as much time as necessary to establish trust with that client. They ask good questions and listen closely to the answers. They lean forward and take careful notes. They seek to understand the customer's situation and needs before they make any attempt to talk about their product or service.

The rule is this. "If the customer likes you and trusts you, the details will not get in the way of the sale. If the prospect, however, is neutral toward you, or even worse, negative, the details will trip you up every step of the way."

Identify Needs Clearly

The third habit of top salespeople is that they make a habit of asking questions and identifying the real needs of the prospect relative to what they are selling. Most prospects are not aware that they can improve their life or work situation when they first meet you. This is the reason prospects often say things like, "I'm not interested," or "I can't afford it," or "We're quite happy with our existing situation or supplier."

This is normal and natural. Most products and services you sell are new, different, and offer advantages and benefits the customer is not yet aware of. The more you ask questions about the customer's situation, and link your product to those needs, the more open the customer becomes to learning about your product or service and eventually buying it.

Take Care with Your Presentation

The fourth habit developed by all sales professionals is the habit of making excellent, logical, well thought out presentations of the features and benefits of their product. Once they have clearly identified the customer's wants and needs, they show the customer that those needs can be ideally satisfied by their product or service, and in a cost-effective way.

In reality, the sale is actually made in the presentation. If you have identified a prospect who can benefit from what you sell, established a comfortable level of trust and rapport, and identified needs clearly, the presentation is where you show the customer why it makes excellent sense to take action on your recommendations.

Friend, Advisor, Teacher

In effective selling, you position yourself as a friend, an advisor, and a teacher. As a friend, you make it clear that you are more concerned with helping the customer solve a problem or satisfy a need than you are about simply making a sale. Once the customer realizes he or she can trust you and what you say, the customer will relax and open up. He or she will then tell you everything you need to know to help him or her make a buying decision or determine that your product or service is probably not appropriate at this time.

As an *advisor* in the sales presentation, instead of trying to overwhelm resistance, you instead present what you are selling as a solution to a problem or as the satisfaction of a need. You present your product or service by giving advice that helps the customer understand why what you sell will improve life or work situations. You invite comments and make recommendations, rather than attempting to induce the customer to buy.

Finally, you position yourself as a teacher by educating your customer in how he or she can most benefit from what you are selling. The more you learn about the customer's situation and teach about the benefits of your product or service, the more the customer will relax, trust you, and accept your recommendations.

Answer Objections Effectively

The fifth stage of excellent selling is the habit of answering objections and resolving concerns in a confident, competent manner. You do this by thinking through all the objections that a qualified prospect might give you for not proceeding with your offer. You then develop logical and complete answers to each of these objections so you are prepared if and when they come up.

The very best sales professionals have thought through every possible objection they could receive and developed completely clear, "bulletproof answers" so that when the objections arise, they can be put to rest quickly.

Ask for the Decision

The sixth part of selling is developing the habit of asking the customer to make a buying decision. No matter how good your presentation or how high the level of trust and credibility that exists between you and your customers, there is always a moment of stress or tension at the making of a buying decision. Your job is to move quickly and professionally through that stressful moment by asking for the order in a confident, professional manner and then wrapping up the sale.

The very best sales professionals plan their closes in advance. They watch for buying signals from the customer. They ask questions to make sure there are no lingering objections. They then ask clearly and straightforwardly for a buying decision and for the customer to take action now.

Here's an interesting point: the more competent and confident you are in asking for the order at the end of the sales presentation, the more motivated and positive you are about prospecting at the beginning of the sales process. The better you get at closing the sale, the better you become at every other stage of the sales process because you develop the habit or the "conditioned response" of anticipating sales success as the result of your efforts. You become self-motivated.

Ask for Resales and Referrals

Finally, top sales professionals develop the habit of asking for resales and referrals from each customer. They know that every person they talk to knows at least 300 other people by first names. They therefore give good service to their customers and ask for referrals to similar prospects.

The habit of thinking in terms of resales and referrals is the key to high income and high profitability. The most successful salespeople and companies have high levels of repeat business and a continuous stream of new customers that come from referrals from their satisfied customers.

Here is an exercise for you. Imagine that three months from today, a law was going to go into effect that made it illegal for you to prospect for new customers. The only selling you could do would be to referrals you received from your existing customer base. You would have to organize your time, your work, and your activities in such a way that your existing customers were so happy with you that they would give you a steady stream of referrals.

What could you do, starting today, to work "by referral only?" What steps could you take immediately to assure that your existing customers supply you with an endless stream of referrals in the future? What should you do right now to begin this process?

The key to success in business is repeat customers. These are customers that buy from you, buy again, and bring their friends. These are people who become "customer advocates." They tell everybody they know about how good your products and services are and urge them to buy from you.

THE KEYS TO PROFITABILITY

In the Profit Impact of Market Strategy (PIMS) studies at Harvard, examining the sales and profitability of 620 companies over a multiyear period, they found that "perceived product quality" was the critical determinant of the sales, growth, and profitability of almost every company.

In addition, they discovered that product quality was only 20 percent determined by the actual product or service itself and 80 percent determined by how the customer was treated during the sales and ownership process. The nicer, more responsive, and more efficient the people in the company were toward the customer, the higher the level of customer loyalty and the greater perceived quality of the product or service sold.

SUPERB CUSTOMER SERVICE

The habit of service orientation toward your customers is the key to repeat sales, lower marketing and sales costs, and higher profitability. There are four habits you need to develop to achieve a reputation for superb customer service: meeting customers' expectations, exceeding their expectations, delighting you customers, and amazing your customers.

Meet Your Customers' Expectations

The first level of service is for you to develop the habit of consistently meeting the expectations of your customers. To achieve this, it is absolutely essential that you find out what customers expect of you. It is vital to your survival and success that you meet those expectations every single time.

A primary source of anger, frustration, and negative emotions, both personally and commercially, is "frustrated expectations." This is when we expect something to happen, but it does not happen the way we wanted it to. Whenever you experience negative emotions of any kind, it can almost always be traced to having been frustrated or disappointed in a particular expectation. This is doubly true with regard to customers and their dealings with different companies.

The most successful and profitable companies are those that made a habit of clearly identifying what customers expect and then organizing the entire business to be sure those expectations are delivered 100 percent of the time.

Exceed Your Customers' Expectations

Meeting customer expectations is enough to keep you in business, but not enough for you to grow and succeed in a competitive marketplace. To do that, you must develop the habit of exceeding customer expectations. You must do more than customers expect, things that are outside of the range of expectations. These extra things you do cause customers to be happy in dealing with you and cause them to want to buy from you again

What are the little things you can do better, faster, cheaper, and easier that will make your customers glad that they bought from you. Could you offer something extra to your customers? Could you do something that your customers had not thought of? How can you exceed your customer's expectations, every day?

As it happens, as soon as a company finds a way to exceed customer expectations and it becomes known in the marketplace, your competitors will copy you and duplicate your efforts in an attempt to stay even with you, if not get ahead. Therefore, every time a way of exceeding customer expectations becomes common knowledge in the workplace, it becomes a *normal* expectation of customers. From then on, customers expect to get what was at one time something extra in the normal course of doing business with you.

Delight Your Customers

The third level of customer satisfaction is the habit of delighting your customers. You delight your customers when you do something so unusual that it makes them especially happy. It can be something as little as a follow-up call from a senior executive to a new customer. It can be a call thanking customers for the business and asking them for ideas on how you might improve your services to them in the future. It can be something larger, like a gift of flowers or fruit to a customer who just placed a large order. It can be a thank you card signed by several people in the company. It can be a personal visit by a key executive to a new customer. In every case, these little gestures, which are not particularly expensive, leave a wonderful impression in the customer's mind and dramatically increase the probability that he or she will buy from you again.

Amaze Your Customers

The highest level of customer service is when you develop the habit of amazing your customers: when you do something for them that is so extraordinary they want to run around and tell everybody they know. Develop the habit of continually thinking of things you could do that would amaze your customers. This could change the whole nature of your business.

Some years ago, in the midst of the Federal Express advertising campaign, "When it absolutely, positively has to be there overnight," there was a major blizzard in Colorado that closed down the mountain passes between Denver and the ski resorts to the west. Without reference to his superiors, a Federal Express deliveryman, who was blocked from fulfilling the promise of Federal Express, charted a helicopter to fly over the mountains and deliver Federal Express packages to his key customers.

To get maximum benefit, he telephoned ahead to find out where he could land a helicopter to deliver the packages. The story was picked up by the newspapers and eventually broadcast worldwide. Federal Express spent several thousand dollars for the helicopter but earned millions of dollars in good publicity by amazing their customers with service beyond anything they could ever expect.

LOVE YOUR CUSTOMERS

Perhaps the most important habit you can develop for business success is to think in terms of "loving your customers." Stand back and look at your customers, your products, your services, your marketing and sales efforts, and your business activities. If you genuinely loved your customers—the way you love the most important people in your life—what would you do differently? What changes would you make in your product or service quality standards? What changes would you make in your customer service policies? If you genuinely loved your customers and wanted to please and satisfy them more and better than anyone else, what would be the first thing you could do to demonstrate this?

Nothing happens until a sale takes place. Your ability to put yourself in the shoes of your customers, to treat each customer the way you would like to be treated if the situation were reversed, is the most important habit you can develop for business and financial success. By developing the habit of thinking in terms of marketing, sales, and customer service all the time, you will become better and better in every area. You will achieve all your business, personal, and financial goals and lead the field in your business. You will earn the esteem, loyalty, and respect of everyone inside and outside of your business and become one of the most successful businesspeople of your generation.

Action Exercises

$ Determine your area of specialization—in customers, products, or markets—and make a plan to become the best in that area.

$ Decide upon your area of excellence, your "unique selling proposition," and organize all your marketing and sales efforts around it.

$ Segment your market and determine those prospects who can most benefit from what you do well and who can buy and pay the most readily.

$ Focus and concentrate all your marketing and sales efforts on your very best prospective customers.

$ Position yourself in everything you say and do as the most credible and believable supplier of your product or service to your ideal customer.

$ Treat your customers as if they were the most important people in your business life, because they are.

$ Decide upon the improvements you are going to make immediately to sell and service your customers better than anyone else in your market.

The Golden Rule for every businessman is this:
"Put yourself in your customer's place."

—Orison Swett Marden

9

The Habits of Personal Effectiveness

> The man who succeeds above his fellows is the one
> who early in life clearly discerns his object, and
> towards that object habitually directs his powers.
>
> —EDWARD GEORGE BULWER-LYTTON

*A*BRAHAM MASLOW, THE TRANSPERsonal psychologist, once wrote, "The ultimate end of human life is to become everything you are capable of becoming." Your purpose should be to fulfill your potential as a human being and to accomplish every goal you can possibly set for yourself. Your aim should be to get the very most out of yourself in every area of your life.

Some people accomplish an extraordinary amount with their lives, as opposed to the great majority who accomplish very little. These peak performers or self-actualizers seem to earn more money; have better families, friends, and relationships; enjoy higher levels of health and energy; achieve much higher levels of success, esteem, and prestige in their fields; and live longer, happier lives than the average. This should be your goal as well.

THE DETERMINANT OF HIGH PERFORMANCE

The only difference between the high performers and the low performers is their habits. High performing, successful, happy men and women are those who have taken the time and disciplined themselves to develop the habits that lead them onward and upward in every area of their lives. Unsuccessful, unhappy people, on the other hand, are those who have not yet developed those habits.

The good news is that all habits have been learned and are therefore learnable. You can learn whatever habits and behaviors you consider desirable and necessary. The only limits are the ones your place on yourself. The question is always, "How badly do you want it?"

If you are willing to work on yourself long enough and hard enough, you can form and shape yourself into the kind of excellent person you are designed to be. No matter what you have done or not done in the past, at any time, you can draw a line through your previous life and make the decision that your future is going to be different. You can begin thinking different thoughts, making different choices and decisions, taking different actions, and developing different habits that will lead you inevitably to the successes that are possible for you.

PERSONAL STRATEGIC PLANNING

The purpose of strategic planning in a business is to increase "return on equity," or ROE. Planning is meant to improve the financial results of the business. In the same way, the purpose of personal strategic planning is to increase R.O.E., or "return on energy." It is to increase your "return on life."

The aim is for you to organize and reorganize your life in such a way that you are earning the highest returns on your mental, emotional, and physical equity invested in your life. Your goal is to organize yourself and use your time to achieve the greatest amount of pleasure, satisfaction, and rewards from everything you do, every hour, every day. And this is very much under your own personal control.

Therefore you must develop the habit of personal strategic planning. You invest the time and effort to think through and plan out your life in advance to assure that you get the very most possible in every area.

With personal strategic planning, you develop the habits of future orientation and long-time perspective. These habits enable you to project forward in your life several years and determine exactly what you want to accomplish and where you want to end up at a specific time in the future.

Think Long Term

The greater clarity you have regarding your long-term goals, the better and more accurate decisions you will make in the short term to assure that you achieve your goals on schedule. For example, if you decide that you are going to be a self-made millionaire 10 to 20 years from now, you set that as your long-term financial goal. You then assess your current situation and determine how much you are worth today. You draw a line from where you are today to where you want to be at a certain date in the future. You then plan out a strategy or roadmap of exactly how you are going to get to your goal in the time that you have allotted.

The rule is this: Be clear about the goal, but be flexible about the process. Be open to the fact that a thousand things will change on the road to your long-term goal. As long as your goal is clear, you can continue to remain flexible and open-minded. You can reevaluate and try different things. You can accept feedback and self-correct. You can go over, around, and through obstacles, and even change and go in a completely different direction. This is the normal and natural process of getting from wherever you are to any long-term goal.

Review Your Goals Daily

Develop the habit of regular goal setting. As I suggested earlier, get a spiral notebook and rewrite your current goals every morning before you start out, in the present tense, as though they were already realities, This exercise programs your goals deeper and deeper into your subconscious mind and causes all kinds of remarkable things to happen that move you toward your goals, sometimes by the most remarkable of coincidences.

The habit of daily goal setting seems to act like a turbocharger on your potential, moving you more rapidly toward your goals than you ever thought possible. When you practice this technique for 30 days, your entire life will change in a very positive way. One month from now, you will be amazed at what has happened to you.

The Ten Goal Exercise

Here is my favorite exercise in personal strategic planning. It launches the whole process of goal setting and leads to remarkable results. Wherever I go in the world—and I've conducted seminars in 24 countries—I give this exercise to my seminar participants: "Take out a sheet of paper, write down ten goals for the next year in the present tense, and then put it away, like a Christmas wish list."

When I return to those cities and countries, I meet people who have taken this advice. They come up to me at my seminars all over the world, to tell me that this simple exercise of writing down their ten goals just *once* has changed their lives. They have often put the list away and not looked at it for a year. When they take it out several months or a year later, they are amazed at how many of their goals have been achieved in that time period.

Writing your goals down just once programs them into your subconscious mind and activates your superconscious faculties. Writing and rewriting them each day is even more powerful. When you write down your goals every single day, you get 10 times, 20 times, 50 times, and even 100 times the impact of writing them down once. Your mind will be stimulated into producing incredible ideas to help you achieve your goals. You will activate the Law of Attraction and begin attracting people, circumstances, ideas, and resources into your life that help you in the most remarkable ways.

By the Law of Correspondence, your outer world will start to become a reflection of your inner world. Without even trying, you will begin thinking about your goals most of the time. The more you think about your goals, the faster you will move toward them, and the faster they will move toward you. Your whole life will change for the better. Only about 3 percent of adults have written goals and plans, and that 3 percent seems to accomplish more than all the others put together.

THINK ON PAPER

One of the most important habits you can develop to increase your return on energy is the habit of thinking on paper. Always have a pen in hand when you think, plan, and organize. Writing things down clarifies your thinking and crystallizes your ideas.

There is something miraculous that happens between the head and the hand. The very act of writing something down activates your visual, auditory, and kinesthetic senses. You see it, you say it to yourself, and you physically write out the words. These three modalities in combination seem to impress what you are writing deeper and deeper into your subconscious mind. This has an ever-greater impact on your thinking, feeling, and behavior afterwards. Most successful people think on paper. Most failures do not.

Start Each Day with a List

Develop the habit of beginning each day with a list of everything you have to do that day. The very best time to make out your daily list is the night before, at the end of the working day. This allows your subconscious mind to work on your list of activities all night long while you are sleeping. Often you will wake up in the morning with insights, ideas, and answers to your problems as a result of programming this list into your mind before you go to sleep.

Develop the habit of setting clear priorities on your list before you begin work. Instead of hurling yourself at the day, like a dog chasing after a passing car, take a few minutes to organize your list. Determine the tasks and activities that will give you the highest return on energy for the amount of time you invest.

FIVE QUESTIONS TO KEEP YOURSELF FOCUSED

Here are five questions that you can ask over and over again until they become a habit, guiding you to always using your time at the very highest level.

Why Am I on the Payroll?

First, ask, "Why am I on the payroll?" What have I been hired to accomplish? What specific measurable results are expected of me at my work? If I were trying to explain to someone else why they pay me money at my job, what reasons would I give?

Most people fall into the habit of thinking that, because they are at work, they are working. They confuse activities with accomplishments. They are often busy all day doing more and more things of lesser and lesser importance. At the end of the day, they claim to be exhausted or stressed out, but they have accomplished very little. They fail to ask themselves, "Why am I on the payroll?"

What Are High-Value Activities?

Second, develop the habit of asking, "What are my highest value activities?" What are the most important things you do each day in your work? If you were to take a list of all of your activities, tasks, and potential results to your boss, and ask your boss to select the three most important things you do, what would you hear?

If you are your own boss, remember there are usually three tasks or activities that account for 90 percent or more of the value that you contribute to your work or business. Almost everything else you do is a support activity for those three tasks. Most of your activities are tasks you think you need to do, in order to do the things for which you are actually paid, and which have the highest value. What are the three most valuable things you do in your work?

You and Only You?

Third, develop the habit of asking the question, "What can I, and only I, do that if done well, will make a real difference?" The answer to this question is something you—and only you—can do. If you don't do it, it will not be done by someone else. But if you do it, and you do it well, it can make the greatest single contribution to your work and to your company at that moment. What is it?

What One Thing?

Fourth, develop the habit of asking this question, "If I could only do one thing all day long, what one thing do I do that contributes the greatest value to my company?" If you were to list everything you do on a piece of paper, you would find one task that—if you did it consistently, well, repeatedly all day long—would contribute more value than any of your other tasks, or even all of your other tasks put together.

What one task or activity that is the highest use of your talents and abilities would contribute the very most to your work and your life if you could do it all day long? How could you organize your time and your work so you focus more and more on this single task?

One of the most important keys to personal effectiveness is for you to develop the habit of spending more time, and becoming more skilled, at those few activities that contribute the greatest value to your work. Everything else you do is usually of lower value than these essential tasks.

What Is Your Best Use of Time?

Fifth, and perhaps, the most important characteristic in personal management is the habit of asking, "What is the most valuable use of my time, right now?" There is always an answer to this question, for every minute and every hour. Your ability to accurately ask and answer this question is the key to high performance, maximum productivity, personal effectiveness, and great success.

In its simplest terms, people succeed because they develop the habit of consistently working on the one thing that can give them the highest rate of return on energy—and life—out of all the possible things they could be doing at the moment. People fail because they are unable or unwilling to

Double Your Income, Double Your Time Off

In my coaching and mentoring programs, I promise my clients that they will learn how to double their incomes and double their time off over the course of the 12-month program. Recently, at the second session of the program, which was 90 days after the first session, Joanne stood up and told the group her story.

"Three months ago, when I first attended this program, I told Brian privately that I did not believe that it was possible for me to double my income and double my time off. My situation was that I have been working for an entrepreneurial business for eight years, putting in 10 to 12 hours per day, five and six days per week. I was not spending enough time with my husband and my two children, and this was causing me an enormous amount of stress. But I saw no way out."

"Brian told me to make a list of all the things that I do in my work over the course of a month. I came up with 16 items. Without looking at the list, Brian told me to ask the key question, 'If you could only do one thing on your list, all day long, which one activity would contribute the greatest value to your company?'"

I quickly identified the one thing that I do that seems to contribute the greatest value. He then asked me to identify items number two and three, asking the same question. Then, again without looking at the list, he said those three items would account for 90 percent or more of all the value I contribute to my company. Everything else could be delegated or outsourced to other people. As I reviewed the list, I saw that he was right."

"The next Monday morning at 10:00 A.M., I sat down with my boss and I told him about the analysis I had done on my work. I told him that I needed his help to delegate, outsource, or eliminate the 13 items on my list of low value so that I could spend all my time working on the top three items. If I could focus on these three tasks, I told him, I believed that I could double my productivity and my value to the company. And if I was successful, and doubled my value, I would like to be paid twice as much."

"My boss looked at the list and then looked up at me. 'You are absolutely right,' he said. 'I'll help you delegate and outsource all these low-level tasks to free you up to work on your three top tasks. They are the things you do that make the greatest difference around here.'"

Joanne went on to say, "The bottom line is that he did, and then I did. Within 30 days, I had cut my work week down to eight hours per day, five days per week, and I was producing more than twice as much as I ever had before. My income doubled, and my time with my family doubled as well. It was an absolutely amazing process."

---

determine their true priorities or because they are not disciplined enough to work on their key tasks exclusively until they are complete.

GET CONTROL OF YOUR TIME AND YOUR LIFE

One of the habits of personal management is for you to continually focus on those few things that only you can do, that if done well, will make a real difference at work. Simultaneously, you must continually use your creativity, not to find ways to do more things, but to find ways to eliminate, downsize, and outsource tasks that contribute very little to your life or work.

The fact is, you can get control over your time and your life, and increase your productivity, performance, and output, only to the degree to which you *stop doing things* of low value. This is the only way that you can free up more time to do those few things that really make a difference.

Develop the habit of continually questioning every task and asking:

- Does this task have to be done at all?
- Does this task have to be done by me?
- Does this task have to be done now?
- Is there anyone else who can do this task almost as well as I can?"

Whenever possible, delegate or outsource the task to someone else so you can focus on the few things that only you can do that will really make a valuable contribution to your work.

PRACTICE THE ABCDE METHOD

In setting priorities so that you can increase your return on energy, develop the habit of applying the ABCDE Method to your work list each day before you begin. In using this method, develop the habit of thinking through the possible consequences of doing or not doing a particular task. A task for which there are serious potential consequences is a high priority task. A task for which there are very few consequences is a low priority task. The measure of consequences is the key determinant of whether or not it is something that you should do now, later, or not at all.

Review your list of activities and place an A, B, C, D, or E next to each one.

An "A" task is something that you must do. There are serious consequences for doing it or not doing it. Completion of this task is essential to your success in your work or personal life. Identify all the A tasks on your list. If you have more than one A task, organize them by priority as A-1, A-2, A-3, and so on.

A "B" task is something that you should do. It needs to be done at some time. If you do not do this task, someone will be inconvenienced or unhappy, but there are only mild consequences for completion or non-completion. The rule is that you should never do a B task when an A task is still left undone.

A "C" task is something that would be *nice* to do, but that has no consequences at all, to you or anyone else. In other words, it doesn't really matter if the task is done or not. You should never do a C task when you have a B task left undone, just as you should never do a B task if you have an A task undone.

A "D" task is something that you can and should delegate to others. The rule is that you should develop the habit of delegating everything that can possibly be done by others, in order to free up more of your time for the few things that only you can do.

An "E" task is something that you can and should *eliminate* as quickly as possible. You can only get control over your time to the degree to which you eliminate everything of low value and no value so that you can focus on just those things that really make a difference in your life and work.

Your most powerful tool for success is your ability to think. Nowhere is this ability more important than when you use it to choose and decide what you are going to do, and in what order. The accuracy of your choices in deciding how you are going to spend your time and your life largely determines everything that happens to you. And you are always free to choose.

PRACTICE THE PARETO PRINCIPLE

Develop the habit of applying the 80/20 Rule to everything you do. This rule, first discovered by Vilfredo Pareto in 1895, says that 80 percent of the value of what you do will be determined by 20 percent of your activities in that area.

This means that 20 percent of your prospects will turn into 80 percent of your customers. Twenty percent of your customers will buy 80 percent of your products or services; 20 percent of your products or services will account for 80 percent of your profits. This rule also means that 20 percent of your customers will account for 80 percent of your problems and expenses, as well.

In any list of ten items, two of those items will be worth all the others put together. Make a habit of applying the 80/20 Rule to every part of your business and personal life. Keep focused on doing the 20 percent of items or tasks that are worth several times the value of the other tasks, but that take the same amount of time.

Most people allocate their time across the number of items they have to do. But highly productive people allocate their times based on the value of each task or activity. You should do the same.

OVERCOME PROCRASTINATION

One of the most important personal management habits you can develop is the habit of overcoming procrastination and getting your most important job done first. In my book *Eat That Frog!* (Berrett-Kohler, 2001), which has become a worldwide bestseller, I explain a proven, practical process you can learn to organize your time and your life, select your most important task, begin on that task, and work on it single-mindedly until it is complete.

One of the principles I teach is based on the fact that you become what you think about most of the time. You also become what you say to yourself most of the time. Whenever you find yourself procrastinating, you repeat to yourself, firmly and emphatically, the words, *"Do it now! Do it now! Do it now!"* These words seem to get you refocused and stimulate you back into working on your key task.

The more you discipline yourself to concentrate single-mindedly on your most important task, and stay with it until it is done, the more energy you have. Each time you complete an important task, your brain releases a hormone called a beta-endorphin. This is often referred to as nature's "happy drug." Each time your brain releases endorphins, you feel happy, exhilarated, motivated, positive, and enthusiastic. Endorphins make you feel more positive, creative, and confident. Each time you complete an important task, you get an endorphin rush, which stimulates and motivates you into doing even more.

GETTING THE JOB DONE COMPLETELY

Developing the habit of starting on your most important task and staying with it until it is 100 percent complete is a great time saver, as well. Stretching out a task and working on it piecemeal is a great time waster. Let me explain.

Each task has three parts: first, you warm up and get ready; second, you work on the task; and third, you wind down and put things away. Each time you stop and start a task without completing it, you have to go through a warm-up and a warm-down period that eventually leads to your spending as much as 500 percent of the time necessary to do the task if you were to stay with it until completion.

Develop the habit of disciplining yourself to complete your tasks, whatever they are. Not only will you get more done, but task completion gives you the motivation and energy you need to accomplish even more.

Single-minded concentration on one thing, the most important thing, is one of the most powerful habits you can develop for personal productivity.

THE PERSONAL PRODUCTIVITY FORMULA

There is a productivity formula, like a recipe, that you can learn and practice until it becomes automatic and easy. When you develop the habit of thinking in terms of these seven key ways to increase your output, you can double your productivity, performance, and results in no time at all.

Work Hard

First, develop the habit of working longer and harder than other people, as I mentioned earlier in this book. Start a little earlier, work a little harder, and stay a little later. Work all the time you work. When you start work, don't fool around. Get busy and stay busy all day long. This habit alone can increase your productivity 50 to 100 percent from the first day.

Work Fast

Second, develop the habit of working faster and getting the job done quickly. Pick up the pace. Move more rapidly from place to place and from task to task. Develop a sense of urgency, a bias for action. Become known as the person who gets things done quickly, rather than a person who gets things done when he or she gets around to them.

Work Smart

Third, develop the habit of doing the most important things, as we have discussed throughout this chapter. Remember, every single thing you do has a value that makes it more or less important than every other thing you do. The Law of the Excluded Alternative says, "Doing one thing means not doing something else." Make sure whatever you are doing at the moment is the most important thing you could be doing. Otherwise, you will end up putting more important tasks aside.

The sad fact is, even if you do an unimportant task extraordinarily well, it will have no impact on your career. In fact, spending too much time doing a good job on something of low priority or value can actually damage your career because it keeps you from working on something that really matters. As management consultant Benjamin Tregoe once wrote, "The very worst use of time is to do well what need not be done at all."

Work on Your Strengths

Fourth, develop the habit of working on those things you are better at. There are special talents and skills you have developed throughout your career that enable you to do certain things quickly and well. You make fewer mistakes and therefore save an enormous amount of time in going back and making corrections. The more time you spend doing things you are better at, the better you get at those tasks and activities, and the more of them you get done in a shorter period of time.

What tasks are you the very best at doing in your work? How could you organize your work so you are doing more and more of them at a higher level?

Commit to Excellence

Earlier in my career, I was a copywriter for a large advertising agency. When I decided to get into copywriting, I went to the public library and checked out every book they had on the subject. I read, studied, and practiced writing advertising copy hour after hour, long into the night. When I finally got a job in the field, I wrote and rewrote advertising copy eight to ten hours every day, five days a week, under the close supervision of a senior copywriter.

Today, I can write advertising copy that is clear, hard-hitting, and effective as quickly and as easily as the average person can change the television with a remote control. In my company, I can write excellent copy for our advertisements and brochures faster than anyone else. The same work might take other people many hours to do, at a lower level of quality.

Work More Efficiently

Fifth, develop the habit of bunching your tasks. Take advantage of the learning curve. This principle says the more similar tasks you do, one after the other, the faster you will complete each subsequent task, and at the same or higher level of quality.

For example, dictate all of your letters at once. Write all of your business proposals at once. Clear up all your correspondence, or assemble all of your expenses at the same time. Write all your reports at once. Do all your telephone prospecting at the same time.

Efficiency experts calculate that if you have ten similar tasks to do, and you do them all at once, one after the other, by the time you get to the tenth task, you will be working so efficiently that it will be taking you only 20 percent of the time it took you to do the first item on the list. Bunching your tasks is a powerful personal productivity habit.

Work Better

Sixth, develop the habit of continuously improving and getting better at your key tasks. This is one of the most effective time management principles of all. The better you become at what you do, the more of it you can get done in a shorter period of time. Sometimes, improving in one essential skill can have a multiplier effect, increasing your productivity and performance in many other areas of your work.

For example, if you do not know how to type with a keyboard, you will use the "hunt and peck method." You will type with two fingers, and no matter how long you work at the keyboard, you will only be able to type five to eight words per minute.

However, if you decide to learn to touch-type, you could get any one of several popular touch-typing computer programs, practice 20 to 30 minutes each day, and within 90 days you will be touch-typing at 50 to 80 words per minute. You will have increased your productivity, performance, and output in typing by 1,000 percent. You will have opened up the entire world of the Internet for yourself by the development of a single skill, which is learnable by anyone.

The Value of Preparation

Some time ago, I was asked by the executive vice president of a large company to attend the annual business meeting and lead the group through a strategic planning exercise. As it turned out, this company had a very headstrong and dominating president who took over every discussion of strategy and dominated it, allowing little or no input from the other executives present. As a result, people were demoralized, and the company was floundering in the marketplace.

I was to be introduced as a "surprise" to the president and the team of senior executives. If I were not successful, the consequences for the company could be serious. I therefore asked them to send me the outlines and agendas from their previous executive committee meetings. I received about 200 pages of notes and observations that had been typed up and distributed over the previous year. The amount of information was almost overwhelming.

Nonetheless, I was determined to do a good job. I sat down and spent 12 solid hours reading, reviewing, and taking notes from the discussions that had taken place in the past. I noticed that the president was continually quoting Peter Drucker and Tom Peters to make his points. As it happened, I was intimately familiar with the work of both of these management experts.

When the meeting began, everyone took his or her places around a large U-shaped table. The executive vice president who had brought me in stood up and introduced me and told everyone, including the president, that he had invited me in to facilitate the discussion. Everyone looked at each other and at the president, and then back to me. The room was full of tension.

The Moment of Truth

I stood up and thanked them for inviting me. I told them I had carefully studied the notes of their proceedings and discussions from the previous year and addressed each of the key executives by name, having taken the time to memorize the names and backgrounds prior to the meeting. Finally, I looked right at the president, who was standing up now, ready to intervene, and told him "I have always been a big fan of Peter Drucker and Tom Peters."

The president stopped where he stood and looked at me with amazement. I then quickly mentioned several books from each writer that I had read and studied thoroughly. There was silence in the room while everyone waited for the president to react. He sat back down in his chair and said, "Great! You take over the meeting."

The outcome of that session, and subsequent sessions, was very productive. We accomplished an enormous amount and achieved tremendous success in formulating a new strategic plan. The tension and stress that had been disrupting the group disappeared. Everyone became happy and relaxed. The entire group became highly cohesive and productive. Afterward, a couple of the executives came up to me and said, "You probably saved this company."

Preparation was the key. Whenever I think of the amount of time and effort that is necessary to prepare for any speech, seminar, meeting, or strategic planning session, I remind myself of that experience.

What one skill could you develop that could help you use more of your other skills at a higher level? If you could be absolutely excellent in any single skill, which one skill would have the greatest positive impact on your career and your income? What can you do, starting today, to develop that skill? Whatever it is, set it as a goal, make a plan, and then work on improving yourself in that area every day until you have mastered the skill and made it part of your personal skill set.

Prepare for Work

Seventh, to get the most out of yourself and your life and to increase your return on the investment of your time, you should develop the habit of preparing thoroughly for every meeting and interview, both inside your company and with people on the outside. Thorough preparation takes a little time at the beginning but can lead to tremendous savings of time later on.

Customers always know when a salesperson is thoroughly prepared. Juries always know when the lawyer is thoroughly prepared. Prospective employers always know when the applicant is thoroughly prepared. Make it a habit to do your homework and get all of your ducks in a row prior to any meeting of importance or significance. Sometimes, the element of preparation is the critical factor that enables you to impress everyone present and achieve great success.

No Such Word

Not long ago, I was preparing to give testimony in a large lawsuit in Los Angeles. I met with the senior trial lawyer for several hours. At the end, he turned over a box full of materials to me and said, "I hope you will have a chance to read through this material before you testify."

I replied, "I always believe in preparing thoroughly for every important meeting. In fact, I believe in *overpreparing*."

He looked me straight in the eye, smiled, and said, "I do not believe there is such a word."

I learned later that he was one of the most skilled and highest paid lawyers in the United States. In that one case alone, he went on to save his client more than $300 million dollars as the result of his commitment to not only preparing, but to "overpreparing." You should do the same.

The wonderful advantage of developing the habit of thorough preparation, and doing your homework prior to every meeting, is that it gives you a tremendous sense of confidence and competence when you go in. It gives you a psychological edge that enables you to perform at your best. It often wins you great business and personal victories that change the whole direction of your life.

BE ON TIME EVERY TIME

Another important habit for you to develop is the habit of punctuality. Less than 5 percent of people are punctual every single time. And everybody knows who they are. They stand out. They are admired and respected by others. Opportunities open up for them. They are considered to be more valuable and more competent than others simply as the result of habitual punctuality.

Legendary football coach Vince Lombardi, when he took over the Green Bay Packers, found that the players often arrived at the bus after the scheduled time of departure. He therefore initiated what he called "Lombardi Time." This was 15 minutes before the scheduled time. From that day forward, if the bus was leaving at 10:00 A.M., everyone was expected to be on the bus by 9:45 A.M. If they weren't, the bus left without them. This only had to happen once for the players to get the message.

Remember, anything that you do repeatedly, over and over, soon becomes a new habit. Resolve that, "Just for today, I am going to be punctual for every meeting." Don't try to change your whole life at one time. Live in what Dale Carnegie called "watertight compartments." Focus on changing one behavior at a time, one day at a time, until it locks in and becomes permanent.

Resolve to be punctual to your very next appointment or meeting. Then, resolve to be punctual for the next meeting as well. Do this, one meeting or event after another until it begins to become automatic and easy. In no time at all, you will have developed the habit of punctuality. Other aspects of your life will seem to change and improve at the same time.

DETERMINE YOUR LIMITING FACTOR

An important key to personal productivity is for you to develop the habit of determining the constraint that sets the speed on the achievement of a particular goal in any area of your life. Begin by identifying a goal that you want to achieve. This can be a financial, personal, or health goal. You then ask, "What factor sets the speed at which I achieve this goal?"

For example, if you want to increase your sales, the constraint or bottleneck on increasing your sales could be the number of prospects you talk to each day. If this is your key constraint, focus all your creativity and energy on alleviating this constraint. Focus on organizing your time and activities so that you increase the number of people you see each business day.

In your business, your goal can be the attainment of a particular financial result. What sets the speed at which you achieve it? It is essential that you identify the correct constraint before you focus on alleviating it. Jim Collins, in his book *Good to Great*, points out how important it is for you to identify the correct "economic denominator" in your business. This is the critical number that determines the success or failure of a particular activity or of your entire enterprise.

For example, your limiting factor in increasing your sales might not be the number of prospects that you speak to, but the quality of each of those prospects. By applying the four marketing principles we discussed earlier, you could identify prospects with far higher likelihoods of buying sooner than other prospects.

Perhaps it is your basic sales skills that are at issue. Perhaps the critical constraint on increasing your sales revolves around your ability to make an effective sales presentation and to get the customer to take action. If this were the answer, the solution would be for you to focus your creativity and energy on upgrading your sales skills, rather than frantically flailing around to get in front of more people.

Doubling the Number of Purchases

The best restaurants have identified the critical constraint to business growth. It is not the amount of food or drink each person consumes; this is largely fixed. No matter how artful the marketing or how polite the waiter, people are not going to eat or drink much more than they already do.

Instead, the critical constraint in business growth for a restaurant, and for many other businesses, is how often customers return to the restaurant in the course of the year. One of my restaurant clients found that the average guest was visiting the restaurant every two months. They then designed a program of customer service and satisfaction that was so effective that people began visiting the restaurant more often. First they came an average of once every six weeks, then once every four weeks.

By using this strategy, my clients were able to double and triple the sales and profitability of their restaurants without the expensive advertising that would be necessary to attract new diners to the restaurant in the first place. Repeat business, rather than new business, was the key to greater success.

Look into Yourself

Look at your own life and work. Ask yourself, "What are the factors that determine how rapidly I achieve my most important goals?"

The 80/20 Rule seems to apply to the subject of constraints in a special way. You will find that fully 80 percent of the constraints or limitations that are keeping you from achieving your goal are within yourself, not in the world around you. They are contained in your own attitudes, beliefs, fears, or lack of a particular skill or quality. Only 20 percent of your constraints are external to you or to your business.

Develop the habit of looking into yourself for the solutions to your problems. Ask this question, "What is it in me that is holding me back from achieving this goal?"

What could it be? Whatever it is, identify it clearly, set a goal to overcome the limitation or develop the habit, and then take action on it every day until you are successful. As the Greek historian Herodotus wrote, "When a man's fight begins with himself, then he is really worth something."

CHANGE YOUR THINKING ABOUT TIME

When I was a young man, I would read an occasional book or article on time management. At that time, I had the idea that my life was like the sun and time management was like one of the planets that orbited around my life. The great change for me came when I realized that time management was the sun of my life, and everything else that happens to me was like planets in orbit around the way I use my time. This insight had a profound influence on my life and work.

The rule is: "If you improve the quality of your time management, you improve the quality of your life."

Make it a habit to read about time management on a regular basis. Make it a habit to listen to audio programs on time management and to use a good time planner or Palm Pilot. Make it a habit to attend at least one time management program or seminar each year.

The fact is, you cannot become "too good" at time management. Every single method, technique, or strategy that you learn, apply, and develop into a habit will have an immediate positive effect on your life. When you develop a set of time and personal management habits that become automatic and easy for you, from morning to night, you will increase your productivity, performance, output, and income by two, three, or even ten times. You will put your career on the fast track in life. You will get more and more done, in less and less time, at a higher and higher level, and earn more and more money.

Great success in whatever field you choose is simply a matter of developing the habits that are consistent with the achievement of extraordinary results. And all habits are learnable.

Action Exercises

$ Begin each day by rewriting your goals, in the present tense, in a spiral notebook. This programs them into your subconscious mind.

$ Plan each day in advance, preferably the night before, by making a list of everything you have to do.

$ Organize your daily work list by priority, using the 80/20 Rule, the ABCDE Method, or both.

$ Overcome procrastination by starting in first thing on your most important and valuable task.

$ Practice single-mindedly on each task, disciplining yourself to work at it non-stop until it is complete.

$ Resolve to be punctual for every appointment and to complete every task before the promised deadline.

Action Exercises, continued

$ Prepare thoroughly for every important meeting; do your homework in advance so you are always ready for anything that happens.

I could never have done what I have done without
the habits of punctuality, order and diligence,
without the determination to concentrate
myself on one subject at a time.

—CHARLES DICKENS

10

The Habits
for Getting Along
Well with Others

> For true love is inexhaustible: the more you give,
> the more you have. And if you go to draw at the
> true fountainhead, the more water you draw,
> the more abundant is its flow
>
> —ANTOINE DE SAINT-EXUPERY

*F*ULLY 85 PERCENT OF YOUR HAPPINESS IN life is going to come from your relationships with other people, according to Sidney Jourard, psychologist and author of *Healthy Personality* (Prentice Hall, 1980). As Aristotle said, "Human beings are social creatures." We live within the context of the people in our lives. How well we get along with them, and they with us, largely determines the quality of everything that happens to us.

Your most important goal in life is to assure your own happiness. If you do not place your own happiness as the central organizing principle of your own life, no one else will do it for you. Each person is intensely focused on doing the things that make him or her happy. As much as we care about the happiness of others, in a natural, automatic, and instinctive way, our happiness always seems to take precedence over the happiness of anyone else.

YOU CAN GIVE AWAY ONLY SOMETHING YOU HAVE

Often, unhappy people say they are sacrificing their own happiness so they can make others happy. But the rule is, "You cannot give away what you don't have. You cannot make other people happy if you are unhappy yourself."

If you want to have happy children, be a happy parent. If you want happy employees and co-workers, be a happy boss and colleague. If you want to have happy customers, be a happy salesperson. If you want to improve the quality of the life of anyone else, begin by improving the quality of your own inner life.

MAKE OTHERS FEEL IMPORTANT

One of the *1,001 Tales of the Arabian Nights* tells the story of a treasure cave that could only be opened if the person said the magic words, "Open Sesame!" At that sound, the vast wall would move aside, and unlimited treasures would be revealed and available to the person who had uttered the magic words.

In putting people first, the "Open Sesame!" of human relationships is to "make others feel important." Making others feel important satisfies the deepest subconscious cravings of human nature. Everything you do or fail to do can be judged against this standard. Does it make people feel more important or less important? That is the question.

Sometimes I ask my audiences, "What percentage of the time are people emotional, and what percentage of the time are people logical?" They respond with various answers and proportions. But the true answer is that people are 100 percent emotional. People decide emotionally and then justify logically. But emotion comes first.

With regard to your emotions, the rule is once more that "Everything counts!" Everything that happens in your life affects you emotionally in some way. Everything that affects you makes you happy or sad, motivated or unmotivated, loving or angry, fearful or confident. Nothing is neutral.

Fearless and Spontaneous

In Chapter 1, we talked about the fact that infants come into the world with no fears at all. They are completely unafraid and spontaneous. Almost every fear that a person has as an adult has been taught to them as a child, primarily as the result of destructive criticism, physical punishment, or the withholding of love.

Very early in life, we begin to develop the fears of failure and criticism. These negative habit patterns then become the root causes of all of our other fears, doubts, and misgivings.

Our parents start the core fears that affect us throughout our lives—those of failure, loss, ridicule, embarrassment, ill health, and death—when they use a combination of destructive criticism and disapproval to manipulate and control our behaviors. We interpret this treatment as the withdrawal of love. Because this loss of love is so traumatic for us, we lose our fearlessness and spontaneity and instead conform to what we think they want so we will be safe.

Because our minds and emotions are largely unformed at an early age, we are easily susceptible to the negative influences of the important people in our lives. When our parents punish us, criticize us, or say negative things to us or about us, we accept their statements as true and valid assessments of who we really are inside. We have no ability to discriminate, question, or reject their words and their treatment of us.

As adults, we continue to have doubts, fears, and misgivings that are rooted in early childhood experience. No matter how much we accomplish later on in life, we are subject to those negative habit patterns that were programmed into us when we were young. Almost any negative experience can trigger the old negative emotions, like habits that have slipped into our subconscious minds, never really disappearing.

Become a Relationship Expert

On the other hand, because we are primarily emotional, we are positively affected by people who say and do things that make us feel important and valuable. Everything a person does or says that raises our self-esteem and feelings of personal value causes us to like and respect ourselves more, and makes us feel happier about ourselves. As a result, we feel positive toward the person who is saying and doing the things that make us feel better about ourselves.

Your job is to become a "relationship expert" by developing the habits of speaking and acting that make people feel important and valuable. When you develop the habit of doing and saying the things that cause people to feel good about themselves, their lives, their work, and families, all kinds of doors will open up for you. You will be welcomed everywhere you go. People will like you and respect you and want to be around you. They will want to hire you, promote you, work for you, and buy from you. They will accept your influence and leadership and give you power and position in your work and in your community.

The good news is, "Everything you do or say that causes another person to feel better in any way also causes you to feel better to the same degree." When you motivate, encourage, or inspire someone else, you feel motivated, encouraged, and inspired yourself. Everything you do to raise the self-esteem of others raises your self-esteem as well.

As it happens, the reverse is also true. Everything you do or say that hurts another person, makes them feel less important, or lowers their self-esteem also has the same effect on you. This is why most negative people always seem to be angry and unhappy. They suffer from low self-esteem. They have negative self-images. They are frustrated and difficult to get along with. They are ineffective in their human relations and usually poor at their work. Everything they do or say that hurts another person in any way also hurts themselves.

Practice the Golden Rule

The starting point of becoming a relationship expert is to develop the habit of practicing the golden rule in everything you do with everyone you meet. The golden rule, which is the one principle many religions have in common, says, "Do unto others as you would have them do unto you."

In Buddhism it says, "Do not do unto others what is hateful to yourself." This principle is so simple—yet so powerful—that if everyone were to apply it, the world would transform overnight.

Dutch philosopher Emmanuel Kant once propounded what he called the "universal maxim." He said, "Live your life as though your every act were to become a universal law for all people." In other words, imagine that everyone would do and say the very things that you are doing and saying at that moment.

When you set this kind of standard for yourself, you begin to transform your life. You immediately become a better person.

FOUR GREAT QUESTIONS

There are four great questions you can ask and answer on a regular basis to keep yourself growing and developing on the path of becoming an excellent person. They are as follows:

1. *"What kind of a world would this world be if everybody in it were just like me?"* The failure to ask this question, and the inability to answer "This world would be a better place" is the cause of most of our problems in the world today.

2. *"What kind of a country would my country be if everyone in it were just like me?"* If everyone could answer that this country would be a better place to live if others lived as they did, we could quickly eliminate crime, alcoholism, drug addiction, welfare, corruption, and all forms of behavior that can exist only as long as the vast majority do not engage in them.

3. *"What kind of a company would my company be if everyone in it were just like me?"* If the executives at the hearts of corporate accounting scandals had asked and answered this question on a regular basis, the problems in their corporations would never have occurred. Every day, you should ask and answer this question about yourself and your work habits to see if you can answer in the

affirmative. If not, what could you change immediately to begin becoming the very best person you could possibly be?

4. *"What kind of a family would my family be if everyone in it were just like me?"* If everyone in your family treated everyone else exactly the way that you treat the people in your family, would your family be a happier, healthier, and more loving place in which to live and grow?

When you ask this question of yourself continually, you will find yourself treating the people in your family better and better. As you improve the quality of your family life, your relationships at work will improve as well.

FIVE GREAT HABITS FOR BETTER RELATIONSHIPS

There are five habits you can develop to assure wonderful human relationships, both at home and at work. They are: acceptance, appreciation, admiration, approval, and attention. The first is for you to develop the habit of acceptance, or what is called in psychology "unconditional positive regard."

Each person has a deep subconscious need to be accepted unconditionally and without reservations by other people. When we were children, our parents often manipulated us by offering or withholding love and acceptance. This conditioned us to be extremely sensitive to the opinions and treatment of others toward us as we grew up. As children and teenagers, we would do almost anything to earn—or at least not lose—the acceptance of our playmates and peers. As adults, the acceptance of the important people and even strangers around us can become so vital to us that we will do whatever it takes—even giving up our individuality—in order not to trigger their disapproval.

When you completely and unconditionally accept other people, just as they are, without comment, criticism, or any suggestion that they need to change in any way, you raise their self-esteem and release more of their innate potential for happiness and self-expression. In the movie, *Bridget Jone's Diary*, her friends are all amazed when she describes another man by saying, "He likes me just the way I am." Apparently, none of them had ever met anyone who felt that way.

The very best romances, marriages, and parenting experiences are situations where each person in the relationship, especially the parents and spouses, unconditionally accept the others, with no reservations. Remember, the opposite of acceptance is rejection. The feeling of not being accepted by others triggers a series of negative emotions, fears, doubts, and feelings of inadequacy. Your job is to make a habit of going through life expressing unconditional acceptance toward others. This will make you welcome wherever you go.

The simplest way to express acceptance of another person is simply to *smile* each time you see him or her. It takes 13 muscles to smile and 111 muscles to frown. It is therefore much easier to smile, and much more effective. Each time you smile, you raise the self-esteem of the person you are smiling at. In addition, you release endorphins in your own brain, which makes you feel happier as well. Make a habit of practicing unconditional acceptance with everyone you meet, under all conditions. You will be amazed at the positive effect you have on the people around you.

Develop an Attitude of Gratitude

The second habit you need to develop to become a relationship expert is the habit of appreciation. One of the most powerful ways of thinking you can develop is an "attitude of gratitude." The more appreciative and thankful you are of the good things in your life, the more that they will increase and expand.

Begin each day by appreciating the fact that you are alive, that you have family and friends, that you have health and well-being. Give thanks for the fact that you have a job, opportunities for the future, and a great county to live in. Instead of complaining and criticizing, as most people do, you should focus on what makes you happy and express your gratitude on every occasion.

The two words that most express an attitude of gratitude are the words "Thank you." Develop the habit of saying thank you to everyone for any deed that warrants any thanks at all. Wave and thank people for letting you cut into line in traffic. Thank your spouse for making breakfast and thank your kids for doing their homework. Thank your boss whenever he says or does anything friendly or helpful and thank your staff for their work. Thank people in restaurants and on telephone calls. Make it a habit to generate a force field of thankful energy that goes before you wherever you go.

Every time you thank people for anything they have done or said or for any quality they have demonstrated, their self-esteem goes up. Every time you say thank you and raise the self-esteem of another, your self-esteem goes up as well.

Everybody Likes a Compliment

The third habit you can develop is the habit of admiration. As Abraham Lincoln wrote, "Everybody likes a compliment." Make it a habit to admire the traits, qualities, or possessions of other people. Compliment them when they are punctual. Compliment them for their achievements. Compliment them on their car or clothes or briefcase. When you go to someone's home, compliment the owner on the home in general and on the different rooms, furniture, and decorations.

Admire people's accomplishments, such as their degrees or diplomas. Admire their children and spouses. Admire their offices and their businesses. Compliment the waiter when he or she serves you quickly, "You certainly are fast today!"

Whenever you compliment a person for anything, especially appearance or an article of clothing, her or his self-esteem goes up. The person feels more valuable, important, and happier. And as a result of the "boomerang effect," you feel happier and more positive yourself. Your self-esteem goes up in equal measure.

Build the Self Esteem of Others

The fourth way you can make others feel important is by developing the habit of giving praise and approval, whenever and wherever it can be given. This satisfies another of the deepest needs of each person, the need to feel valuable and respected by others.

When you praise other people, their self-esteem goes up. They are then motivated to repeat whatever it was they did that caused them to earn your praise in the first place. In fact, one of the definitions of self-esteem is "the degree to which a person feels himself to be praise-worthy."

In motivational psychology, praising someone regularly for a positive behavior develops in him or her the habit of engaging in that behavior. This "positive reinforcement" is a powerful and proven way to motivate and manage people. You get more of whatever you praise and approve.

Make it a habit to always praise and approve other people when they do something positive or desirable, and that you want to see repeated. Praise your children for cleaning up their bedrooms. Praise them for doing their homework. Praise them for getting good grades. Praise your spouse for anything he or she does around the house.

My friend, the management author Ken Blanchard, recommends that you go around your office giving "one-minute praisings." What is even more effective in making someone feel important is to praise the person in front of someone else or at a staff meeting. The more you praise people in front of others for something they have accomplished, the greater impact it has on their self-esteem and feelings of personal value. Often, they will remember a public praising for years.

The Rules for Praising Others

The basic rules for giving praise effectively are these: first, praise *immediately*, right after the person engages in the praise-worthy behavior. The faster the praise or positive feedback, the better the person feels, and the greater effect it has in shaping future behavior.

Second, praise *specifically*. Explain exactly what it is that you approve of. The more specific the praise, the greater impact it has on the person's self-esteem and subsequent behavior in that area.

Third, praise *repeatedly*, each time the person does what you want. This is essential for helping a person develop a new habit of some kind.

For example, if you have an employee who comes in late, praise the person when she or he comes in on time. Each time the usually tardy employee arrives punctually or before the designated work time, go out of your way to offer praise and thanks for the punctuality. At the same time, ignore the employee's late arrivals. This sets up a carrot and stick dynamic that eventually leads to punctually all the time.

Once a person has developed a new habit as the result of regular praise and reinforcement, you can then move to "intermittent reinforcement." This means you only need to praise the person now and then for the behavior to keep it in force. So, praise repeatedly to help the person develop a new, positive habit and then praise intermittently to keep the behavior in place.

The Magic of Listening

The fifth habit you need to be a relationship expert is the habit of paying attention to people when they talk. You need to develop the habit of being a good listener.

As it happens, most people are poor listeners. They usually have several things on their minds at the same time and are paying attention to several different subjects while someone else is talking. As a result, they do not hear the other person clearly and often misunderstand and misremember the content of the discussion. This leads to confusion, arguments, accusations, and inefficiencies.

Listening is a discipline you can learn with practice. Several steps you can follow will help you develop the habit of excellent listening.

First, make a decision to develop the habit of being an excellent listener. Second, begin immediately by practicing intense listening when people talk to you. Third, never allow an exception until people begin to compliment you on what a good listener you are.

FOUR KEYS TO EFFECTIVE LISTENING

There are four keys to effective listening. You can read every book and article, listen to every audio program, and take every course on the subject, but they will all boil down to the four key behaviors of an excellent listener. They are: listen attentively, pause before replying, question for clarification, and feed it back in your own words.

Listen Attentively. Lean forward. Listen without interruptions. Focus intently on the mouth and eyes of the person who is speaking. Imagine your eyes are sunlamps and you want to give the other person's face a tan.

Some people believe that rapt attention is the highest form of flattery. Whenever people are intensely listened to, their self-esteem goes up. They feel more important and more valuable. They feel happy inside. As a result, they feel better toward the person who is making them feel this way by listening so attentively.

One of the ways to listen more attentively is to eliminate all distractions when a person wants to talk to you. If you are in your office, put down all paper, have your secretary hold your calls, and eliminate all distractions. If possible, move away from your desk and sit with the person where you can face them directly with no interruptions or anything in the way.

If you are at home and a member of your family wants to talk to you, make a habit of turning off the television, folding up the newspaper, and putting aside anything that could draw your attention away while the other person is speaking. Turn and face the speaker directly. Lean forward. Imagine that listening to this person is the most important thing you could possibly do all day long. Eventually, this will become a habit.

Pause before Replying. The second key to effective listening is for you to develop the habit of pausing before replying. Instead of jumping in with your own comments when the other person takes a breath, pause for three to five seconds, or even longer. Allow a silence in the conversation. This habit of pausing before speaking has three advantages.

First, you avoid the possibility of interrupting the other person if he is just stopping to gather his thoughts before continuing.

Second, when you pause, you demonstrate clearly to the other person that what has been said is important and that you are giving it careful consideration before replying. On the other hand, if the listener immediately jumps in with comments or observations, it is clear he or she was not really listening at all, but was just waiting for a chance to talk.

Third, and most important, when you pause after a person finishes speaking, you actually hear at a deeper level of mind. The words, like water soaking into the earth, soak deeper into your mind, and you actually understand what was really meant with greater clarity.

Never Assume Understanding. The third key to excellent listening is for you to develop the habit of questioning for clarification. Never assume you understand fully what the other person really means especially if there is any chance of misunderstanding. Instead, pause and then ask, "How do you mean?"

This is my favorite question for making sure I thoroughly understand exactly what the person is saying and what message they are trying to convey: "How do you mean?"

Here is an important rule: "The person who asks questions has control." When you ask questions in a conversation, you take control of the conversation. The person who is asking the questions controls the person who is answering the questions.

When you ask the question, "How do you mean?" or "How do you mean, exactly?" you get an opportunity to listen even more. You understand even better. You maintain control of the conversation in a very gentle and professional way.

The rule in conversation is, "Listening builds trust." The more that you ask good questions and listen closely to the answers, the more the other person trusts you, believes you, and is open to your influence.

The very best way for you to build high quality relationships with other people is to ask them good questions and then listen attentively to the answers. Pause before replying. Question for clarification. Seek intently to understand the other person and how he or she is thinking and feeling before you comment yourself.

Feed It Back in Your Own Words. The fourth key to effective listening is to develop the habit of paraphrasing what the person has said before you reply. Feed it back in your own words. Say something like, "Let me be sure I understand what you are saying . . . ."

Two types of listening are very powerful in building high quality relationships. The first is called "listening to help." This is where you merely act as a sounding board, making no effort to comment or give advice. You encourage the person to talk, and you ask questions that help to expand thinking. "Why do you say that? How do you feel about that? How do you mean?" And so on.

Sometimes, what people need more than anything else is an opportunity to talk out their problems or situation with another person who merely nods, listens, and accepts, without commenting or giving advice. Many psychotherapists make an entire career of sitting quietly while the patient talks nonstop for 50 minutes, then collecting their fee, and scheduling the next visit.

The second form of listening is called "reflective listening." This is where you continually paraphrase and feed back the person's thoughts in a new or different way. For example, the person can be complaining about an argument with his or her boss. You would reflect this back by saying, "It seems that when your boss argues with you it really affects your self-esteem."

In both cases, your skillful use of the practice of listening causes people to like and respect you more. As a result, they are much more open to your input, advice, and influence. Good listeners are welcome wherever they go.

DECIDING WHAT'S TRULY IMPORTANT

One of the questions we ask in our seminars is, "What would you do, how would you spend your time, if you learned today that you only had six months left to live?"

Virtually everyone in our courses over the years has no trouble answering that question. They would spend every possible minute with the most important people in their lives. All financial or material considerations would disappear, and only their most important relationships would have any value to them.

The fact is, relationships are everything. Your relationships form a core part of your identify. They have an inordinate impact on who you are, what you do, and everything you become. Most of us determine our place and position in life in relationship to the people around us.

Develop the habit of putting the people in your family ahead of all other considerations. In our busy, bustling world of commerce and activity today, it is very easy for your life to get out of balance. It is quite common for people to start spending more and more time at work and less time with the members of their family or the people in their key relationships.

MAINTAIN BALANCE BETWEEN LIFE AND WORK

To be truly happy, you must make a habit of maintaining balance between your work and your personal life. The first step in achieving this balance is for you to resolve to "work all the time you work." The reason most people feel they are under so much pressure from their work is because they waste most of the working day. But unfortunately, even if you waste time, the work does not go away. It still has to be done some-time, and often it has to go home and get done in the evenings and on the weekends.

There is the story of the little girl who goes to her mother and says, "Mommy, why is it that Daddy brings a briefcase full of work home every night and never spends time with the family anymore?"

The mother tries to explain. "Honey, you have to understand. Daddy can't get all of his work done at work, so he has to bring it home in the evenings."

The little girl looks up at her mother and says, "If he can't get all his work done, why don't they put him in a slower class?"

Maintain Your Priorities

Work all the time you work. Start earlier, put your head down, and work the entire time throughout the day. If you are spending more than 10 per-cent of your time interacting with your co-workers, it is too much. Keep repeating to yourself, "Back to work! Back to work! Back to work!"

When you go home, resolve to be there with your family 100 percent of the time. The most important part of personal relationships is face-to-face contact and communication. Nothing can replace this. Your goal should be to increase the amount of face-to-face communication time you have with your spouse and children each day. This will improve your family life more than anything else you can do, and it doesn't cost a cent.

When you go home at night, resist the temptation to turn on the television and fight for the remote control. Instead, *leave things off.* Leave the television off. Leave the radio off. Leave the computer off. Turn off your cell phone and your pager. Instead, spend the first hour when you get home building the bridges of communication between yourself and the most important people in your life.

Create Quality Time with Your Family

Spouses should spend at least one full hour each day talking together about subjects that have nothing to do with their work or business. If you are not careful, you will slip into the habit of talking about your work as soon as you get home. Once you begin, like starting an engine, you will end up talking about your work throughout the entire evening. As a result, there will never be any talk about the family or other matters.

Children need at least ten minutes of face-to-face contact with their parents each day. Take the time to sit and talk with them. Ask them questions and practice your listening skills. Children have a deep need to communicate with their parents, but they will only do this if they feel their parents are open to them and interested in hearing what they have to say. This is one of your prime jobs—and a habit you need to develop.

Develop the habit of making time every day with the important people in your life, preferably one to one, or on the telephone if necessary. The biggest regret people have at the end of their lives is that they did not spend enough time with their children when they were young or with their spouses when they were working. Don't let this happen to you.

CREATE CHUNKS OF QUALITY TIME

Develop the habit of creating chunks of time to spend with the members of your family. The value of any relationship is determined by the amount of time you invest in that person. Building and maintaining important relationships requires unbroken chunks of time in 30-, 60-, and 90-minute periods, if not longer.

Use your creativity and initiative to create these chunks of time. My wife and I go out for dinner alone at least once per week. We almost invariably go to a restaurant that is at least 30 minutes away. During this time, we simply talk and interact. We never allow the radio or CD player to be on when we are driving together.

When I first got married, I made a firm decision that I would never allow any music, radio, or noise in my car when I was traveling with members of my family. This is one of the best decisions I ever made. Whenever I go somewhere with one of my children, we leave everything off. When you create a sound vacuum inside a car, it will very quickly fill with conversation. When there are no distractions, the passengers almost immediately start talking about themselves, their lives, their concerns, their worries, doubts, and other things. But as soon as you turn on any music in a car, all conversation stops.

Three or four times each year, my wife and I will drive somewhere for the weekend. We will select a destination at least two or three hours away. During this trip, we just simply talk and exchange ideas. These are some of the very best experiences of our lives. Try it yourself and see.

A friend of mine had to drive his 16-year-old daughter to join her friends on a ski trip because she missed the bus. It was a four-hour trip from his home to the ski resort, and there was no radio reception in the area. Instead, they just talked the entire way. He told me afterward that he learned more about what was going on in his daughter's life in that four-hour trip than he had learned in the previous ten years. He was absolutely astonished at the quality of the conversation that poured out when two people get into a car and drive with no music or radio interruption. The experience changed their relationship completely, in a very positive way.

TAKE REGULAR VACATIONS

It is important that you develop the habit of taking weekends away with your spouse and vacations away with your family. The key is to book the vacations in advance and pay for them on a nonrefundable basis. Many people wait until very close to the date before they begin thinking about booking a vacation. At that time, it is very easy to put it off or delay it because of pressing responsibilities. Often, it is hard to find a place to go. It becomes very easy not to go at all.

But if you buy and pay for a vacation, including airfares, hotels, rental cars, and everything else in advance, you will almost always take that vacation.

Our family has been going to Hawaii in the winter every year for 18 years. We have never missed a vacation. One of the reasons for this is that the Hawaiian resorts are so popular that you have to pay for your vacation in full by April if you want it to be confirmed for December. This prepayment serves as a wonderful discipline and assures that we never miss a family vacation together. These family vacations together have been some of the richest and most rewarding times of our lives.

Treat Your Family Members as You Treat Your Best Customers

In all your interactions with the members of your family and others, make it a habit to practice good manners, to be courteous and kind with everyone. Nothing will set you apart as a quality person faster than the habit of being courteous and kind in every situation.

Always say "please" and "thank you." Be patient and wait your turn in conversations. Open the doors for other people, when appropriate. Never criticize, complain, or condemn. Attempt to be gracious and friendly with everybody and in every interaction. Some of the very best and most respected people in our society are men and women who make a habit of being well mannered in everything they do. And you can develop the manners you need by regularly practicing those you most admire in other people.

FORGIVE AND LET GO

Perhaps the most important habit you can develop to have wonderful relationships and live a long and happy life is the habit of forgiveness.

Most every religion and spiritual tradition seems to have *forgiveness* as a core principle for spiritual development. By forgiveness, I mean your ability to freely forgive other people for anything they have ever done or

The Damaged Car

Some years ago, I bought a new Mercedes and left it with my wife when I went off on a business trip. When I called home the following day, she asked, "Are you sitting down? I have something I have to tell you." (By the way, these are not words that you want to hear on the phone when you are away.)

I said, "Yes, I'm sitting down, go ahead."

She said, "I was taking the children to school this morning and one of them left the door open when he got into the back seat. I backed out and hit the garage with your door and smashed it up."

I asked her, "Are you all right? Are the children all right?"

She said, "Yes, we are all fine. The car wasn't moving that fast. But it is going to cost almost $2,000 to fix the door."

I said, "Well, that's too bad, but life goes on."

She said, "Aren't you mad?"

I said, "Did you do it on purpose?"

She said, "Of course not."

"Well then," I said, "why should I be mad? Wives are more important than cars or back doors."

I never commented, criticized, or complained about the accident again. As far as I was concerned, it was a fact. It was a part of the past that could not be changed. It was not worth a single moment of negative emotion or concern.

The point is this: things that have happened in your past are facts that cannot be changed. The desire to have something in your past be different than it actually was is a major reason for negative emotions, anger, resentment, and blame. The cure for these is for you to develop the habit of forgiveness and to let go of every negative emotion and experience that has ever happened to you.

said that has hurt you in any way. The ability to forgive opens the keys to the spiritual kingdom. The ability to forgive frees you from the past and makes you a completely different person. Virtually all negative emotions, anger, frustration, guilt, resentment, envy, jealousy, and blame arise from the inability to forgive a person for something that has been done or said in the past.

Many people go through their entire lives angry and resentful toward one or both of their parents for a mistake their parents made with them at an early age. They are still angry because they felt that one of their parents was unfair, unjust, unsupportive, closed-minded, or unduly critical or hurtful.

It's Time to Move On

Sometimes, I ask my thousand-person audiences, "Is there anyone here who had a difficult childhood, who has had a bad relationship, a bad boss, or a friend or business associate who betrayed or cheated them, or who has otherwise been badly treated in life?"

Almost everyone moans and raises their hands. I then say, "Well, get over it!"

This may sound frivolous or cruel, but it is one of the most important things I've learned in a lifetime of working with more than two million people. Most of your unhappiness comes from your failure to let go of negative experiences from your past. As a result, you keep them alive, like feeding a fire. Not only did you pay a price in terms of pain and hurt when the event occurred, but, you continue to pay that price, over and over again, by keeping the event alive.

Divide Life Situations into Two Categories

It is very important, especially in relationships, that you divide your situations in life into two categories: facts and problems. What is the difference between a fact and a problem? Well, a fact is something that just is. It exists. It is unchangeable. The weather is a fact. Your height is a fact. Your age is a fact. A fact is something that cannot be changed or wished away.

A problem, on the other hand, is something you can do something about. It is amenable to a solution. It represents a situation that can be changed. One of the great rules for success and happiness in life is to refuse to become upset, or remain upset, over a fact.

With regard to life, there are two time periods, the past and the future. The present is a single second moving between them. A past event is not a problem; it is a fact. It is unchangeable. One of the rules for happiness is for you not to worry about things that happened in the past that you cannot change. One of the rules for success in your relationships is to never criticize or complain about something that someone has done that cannot be changed. Be sure to distinguish between the two.

Four People to Forgive

For you to set yourself free and get on with the rest of your life, you need to forgive four people. They are: your parents, people from previous relationships, everyone else, and finally, yourself.

YOUR PARENTS

First, make a habit of forgiving your parents for every mistake they ever made in bringing you up. All parents make mistakes with their children. They do the very best they can, with what they have, based on their own experience, and their current situation; but they make mistakes. This is a fact.

If your parents made a mistake with you, you can say to yourself, "I forgive them completely for everything." And then let it go. If your parents are still alive, go and sit down with them and discuss the events and experiences you still feel angry or resentful about. Tell them, "For a long time, I was angry and resentful about this, but I have decided to forgive you unconditionally and let it go." And then never bring it up again.

It is only when you can freely forgive your parents, and let go of any lingering anger or resentment, that you truly grow up and become an adult. Until that point of forgiveness, you are still a child, seeing yourself as a victim. You are still trapped in the past. Forgiveness sets you free to get on with your life.

OPEN THE JAIL DOORS

The second person you have to forgive is any individual from a previous relationship, especially a romantic relationship or a bad marriage, that you still feel angry about.

Begin by accepting that you were at least 50 percent responsible for what happened. You got yourself into the situation, and you kept yourself in it, long after you began to feel unhappy. Make a decision today to forgive the other person, no matter what he or she did or said, and just let it go. Think about who you are, what you want, and where you want to go in the future, and let the past go. "When you turn toward the sun, the shadows fall behind you."

It takes two people to keep someone in jail, the prisoner and the jailer. When you let the "prisoner" out of the mental jail you have been holding him or her in, you set yourself free as well. As Buddy Hackett, the humorist, once said, "I never hold grudges; while you're holding grudges, they're out dancing!"

ISSUE A BLANKET AMNESTY

The third person you have to forgive is everyone else who has ever hurt you in any way. Forgive your siblings and people from your childhood. Forgive your teachers and early relationships, your bad bosses, and dishonest business partners. Sweep them all together and issue a "blanket amnesty." Forgive every person who has ever caused you any unhappiness in the past. Resolve today to let them go forever. Like dropping a rock into a bottomless pit, open your hand and let those negative experiences disappear. Don't talk about them, think about them, or review them ever again. As far as you are concerned, they are dead issues.

LET YOURSELF OFF THE HOOK

The fourth person you have to forgive is yourself. It is absolutely amazing how many people are still sitting in negative judgment on themselves because of some wicked, senseless, brainless, foolish, or cruel thing they did in the past.

The fact is, your life is a continuous process of growth and evolution. When you did something in the past that you now disapprove of, you were a different person. You were not the person you are today. You are a new person with greater wisdom and experience who would never think of doing what you might have done when you were younger. Let yourself off the hook. Forgive yourself and let yourself go.

There is nothing wrong with making a mistake, or hundreds of mistakes, as you grow and mature. It is virtually inevitable. But it is ridiculous for you not to forgive yourself for those mistakes and get on with the rest of your life.

Set Everyone Free

The wonderful thing about the habit of forgiveness is that it sets you free. It also sets everyone that you forgive free as well. Forgiveness is one of the most uplifting and liberating habits you can develop in all human relationships.

Your goal is to reach the point where you do not feel any anger or resentment toward a single person or event in your life. Whenever you think of a person that may have hurt you, you immediately cancel the thought by saying, "God bless him/her; I forgive him/her for everything." Then get your mind busy with what you want and start thinking about the specific actions you can take to achieve it. Get so busy working toward the things that are important to you that you don't have time to think or worry about the things that happened in the past—things you cannot change in any case.

PUT PEOPLE FIRST

Resolve today to develop the habits of men and women who enjoy wonderful relationships all the days of their lives. Let go of everything that has happened in the past that has hurt you in any way, and instead concentrate on making other people feel important.

Make it a habit to go through life doing and saying the things that raise the self-esteem of others and make them feel valuable. Every kind and generous thing you do or say will boomerang back to you and make you a happier, healthier, more successful person. There are no limits.

Action Exercises

$ Make a list of the most important people in your personal and business life; think of specific things you could do to improve your relationships with these people.

$ Resolve today to make others feel important whenever you can; start at home with the most valuable people in your life.

$ Develop the habit of listening better when you converse with other people; pay close attention, pause before replying, question for clarification, and feed back what they say in your own words.

$ Develop an attitude of gratitude for everything and everyone in your life that you are happy about for any reason. Say "thank you" on every occasion.

$ Give "one minute praisings" to your family members, friends, co-workers, and other people you meet throughout the day.

$ Maintain a healthy balance between your work and your family life; make plans to spend more quality time with the people you care about the most.

$ Practice forgiving everyone and anyone who has hurt you in any way. Let go all past grievances, and get so busy working on goals that are important to you that you don't have time to think about the past.

Treasure the love you receive above all.
It will survive long after your gold and
good health have vanished.

—OG MANDINO

11

The Habits for Health and Well-Being

> March on. Do not tarry. To go forward is to
> move toward perfection. March on, and
> fear not the thorns, or the sharp
> stones on life's path.
>
> —KAHLIL GIBRAN

*T*HERE HAS NEVER BEEN A TIME IN human history where you can live longer and live better than you can today. Incredible advances in pharmaceuticals, medicine, and health care enable people to overcome disease and illness and continue to thrive well into their 70s and 80s. Perhaps the largest growing demographic group in America today is people who are 90 and 100 years old or older. Your job is to join this group and to be fit and healthy all the days of your life.

For almost the entire history of the human race, longevity was a matter of accident or coincidence. Today longevity is a matter of design and choice. You can actually decide today to enjoy superb levels of physical health, and by developing specific health habits, you can assure that you live longer and better than has been possible for any other generation in human history.

Most of the major causes of premature death are preventable to some degree. They include heart disease, cancer, strokes, lung cancer caused by smoking, death from automobile accidents, and death from diabetes often brought on by obesity and poor nutritional habits. To a greater or lesser degree, you can exert tremendous control over your health in each of these areas.

In this chapter, you will learn the health habits practiced by those men and women who are seldom sick, have abundant energy and vitality, and who both survive and thrive into the later decades of life. You will learn how to develop the habits that assure that you live longer and live better than most other people in society around you.

CHOOSE TO BE HEALTHY AND FIT

The first habit for you to develop is the habit of achieving and maintaining your proper weight. More than 50 million Americans today are officially classified as "obese." This means that they are more than 20 percent above their ideal weight based on height and weight charts. Even worse, many millions are officially classified as "morbidly obese," 40 and 50 percent above their ideal weights. They are in danger of dying from being so overweight.

An obese person once complained, "The reason I'm overweight is because of my glands." To which the doctor replied, "Yes, you're right. It is your mouth gland, and it is malfunctioning five times a day."

Everything you are, and ever will be, is the result of your choices and decisions. If you want to change some aspect of your life, you have to make new choices and new decisions and then discipline yourself to follow through on your decisions.

Being overweight is very much a matter of choice. No one can eat for you but yourself. No one can put the food into your mouth for you. You only eat as the result of your own decisions and your own actions. Anyone who is overweight is in that condition because they have been unable to restrain themselves in the presence of food for a very long time.

The Secret of Good Health

There are thousands of diet books and plans. They can all be summarized into one simple five-word rule for proper weight, excellent health, and long life: "Eat less and exercise more."

The only way to achieve your proper weight is to develop the habit of eating less and exercising more each day and each week. But just as it takes you months and years to become overweight, it takes you many months to get rid of the weight once you make that decision.

It is not easy to lose weight. This is because you develop automatic habits of eating that are hard to break. You get into a rhythm of eating certain foods morning, noon, and night. You become accustomed to eating snacks between meals and to overeating in the evening. It is not easy to break these habits, but it is definitely possible. This is your goal.

Set Your Goal for Superb Physical Health

The way to achieve your ideal weight is to first of all set a specific goal for the amount that you want to weigh at a specific time and date. Write it down. Make a list of everything you think you can do to achieve that goal. Then take action on your list and work on achieving this goal every single day until you reach it.

At the same time, create a clear mental picture of yourself as thin, trim, and fit. Take a picture of a body that you admire out of a magazine and glue a photo of your face onto that body. Put this picture on the door of your refrigerator and another similar picture on your bathroom mirror. Feed your mind with this picture of yourself with your ideal body, at your ideal weight, over and over again, until your subconscious mind accepts this picture as a command and begins to influence your thoughts, feelings, and behaviors toward that weight.

Affirm to yourself over and over again, "I weigh X number of pounds. I weigh X number of pounds. I weigh X number of pounds." When you combine visualization and affirmation, plus daily action to achieve and maintain your ideal weight, you will begin moving rapidly toward fitness and health, almost without effort.

Be gentle with yourself. Don't attempt to lose an enormous amount of weight in a short period of time. Just as it takes a long time to gain weight, it takes a long time to lose the weight and keep it off permanently. Resolve to lose one ounce per day, two pounds per month. You can set a higher goal if you like, but the more gradually you take off the weight by adjusting your eating and exercise habits, the more likely it is that you will develop new, permanent habits that will enable you to keep the weight off forever.

Rewire Your Thinking about Food

The primary reason for overweight and obesity is because of the habit of associating food with pleasure. As you know, all human motivation is based on the tendency to move from pain to pleasure, from discomfort to comfort, from dissatisfaction to satisfaction. As a child, you were rewarded with delicious foods and desserts when you cleaned your plate or did something your parents approved of. As an adult, you have now developed the habit of associating happiness with eating delicious things and receiving the approval of others.

In order to achieve your ideal weight, you have to reverse the wires in your subconscious mind. You have to disconnect them and reconnect them so that you get genuine pleasure from eating less and being thin. You must develop a positive association between feeling mildly hungry, eating small portions, and feeling light and trim as a result. When you develop the habit of enjoying the feeling of eating less and exercising more, this habit will grow stronger and stronger over time, and your weight problems will eventually disappear altogether.

EAT THE RIGHT FOODS

The second habit you need to develop for long life full of health and fitness is the habit of eating a proper diet. You have to develop the habit of eating the right foods, in the right proportions, at the right times.

Everyone knows they should eat a more balanced diet, containing more fruits, vegetables, and whole grain products. In addition to this basic principle, there are several things you can do to modify your diet and develop the habits of good nutrition, which will lead to a combination of weight loss and higher levels of energy and fitness.

At the Los Angeles Olympic Games in 1984, athletes from more than 100 countries were studied to find out what their diets had in common. The researchers discovered that even though the athletes' diets consisted of many different foods, they all included a variety of fruits and vegetables, lean source proteins, and large quantities of water. This is the diet for peak performance and Olympic fitness.

The Three White Poisons

In addition to eating a peak performance diet to achieve rapid weight loss and improved functioning, you should develop the habit of eliminating the "three white poisons"—salt, sugar, and flour—from your diet. This change in your diet is so simple and yet so powerful that every one of my students who tries it is absolutely amazed at how quickly they get noticeable results.

A man from Florida wrote to me recently.

I have attended your seminars and listened to your audio programs for years. As a result, I have gone from rags to riches. I moved to the top of my field and became a millionaire over the course of 12 years of hard work. But I still had one problem. I was about 20 pounds overweight and I could not get rid of this excess weight, no matter what I did.

Then one day, in listening to one of your programs, I heard about the importance of eliminating the three white poisons. Within 90 days, I had dropped the 20 pounds, and never put it on again. My self-image improved, and my self-esteem went up. I had to get a whole new wardrobe. Now, every time I look in the mirror I feel wonderful about myself. It changed my life!

The average adult requires about two pounds of salt per year for ideal physical functioning. Unfortunately, the average adult in America consumes almost 20 pounds of salt per year, in a variety of forms. Almost all snack foods, such as peanuts, chips, Fritos, and others, are soaked in large quantities of salt. In addition, many people pour salt on their food before they even taste it.

When you take in more salt than you require, your body has to compensate by retaining water to hold the salt in solution. This causes you to swell up and feel bloated. Not only that, too much salt can contribute to high blood pressure, fatigue, poor digestion, sleeplessness, nervous twitches, and a general feeling of tiredness throughout the day.

When you stop consuming foods that are heavy in salt and stop putting salt on your meals, you will feel better immediately. There is so much salt in the foods you consume that you need no extra salt in your diet. If anything, you get too much salt without even trying.

Eliminate All Sugars

The second white poison is anything that contains sugar of any kind. The excess consumption of sugar is so harmful for you that you can transform how you feel almost overnight by refusing to consume anything that has sugar in it.

When you were a child, you developed the habit of associating sweet things with happiness, pleasure, and rewards. As an adult, you continue to give yourself the same pleasures and rewards by consuming soft drinks, candy, cakes, dessert, and sugars of all kinds, in all sorts of foods.

The average adult requires no extra sugar for adequate functioning and ideal health. But the average adult in America consumes something like 120 extra pounds of sugar over the course of a year. Just by eliminating all products containing sugar and salt, your weight will drop almost immediately.

Develop the habit of eating foods composed of complex carbohydrates. A complex carbohydrate is contained in fruits, vegetables, and whole grain products. These foods contain large amounts of energy, but they must be broken down in the digestive process for that energy to be available. These foods also contain large quantities of vitamins and minerals. In the process of digestion, these vitamins and minerals are released and freed up for your body.

AVOIDING THE SUGAR RUSH

On the other hand, simple carbohydrates, those made of sugar products, require no time to digest at all. They go straight into the bloodstream. This is why you often get a "sugar rush" after consuming a sugar-based product, such as a doughnut or candy bar. Even worse, your glucose or sugar level *spikes* just after you consume a sugar-based food or drink. When your blood sugar level spikes, your body immediately goes onto "emergency" status. It quickly secretes insulin into your system to remove the excess sugar. As a result, in one to two hours, you actually experience an "energy slump." The excess insulin secreted by your body removes so much sugar that you find yourself feeling fatigued and even light-headed a couple of hours after consuming a sugar-based food or drink.

If you continue to consume sugar products, thereby triggering the insulin reaction, you experience energy highs and lows throughout the day. As a result, you will experience greater stress, a decreased ability to concentrate and think clearly, and additional fatigue by the end of the day. Sugar is very much a "poison" that you can eliminate from your diet with no loss of nutrition and a tremendous increase in health, energy, and fitness.

LEARN TO EAT DIFFERENTLY

To put it another way, consuming complex carbohydrates in the form of healthy, nutritious foods is like putting an energy log on your physical fire. It burns long and slowly and generates a consistent, steady flow of energy that enables you to perform at your best. Consuming a food high in sugar is like throwing gasoline on a fire. There is a huge flare-up for a short period of time, and then all the energy is quickly removed from your system, and you are back to feeling tired again.

By the way, most people associate eating sweet things with eating dessert after a meal. What nutritionists have discovered is that for you to feel completely satisfied after a meal, you need to have experienced the tastes of salt, pungency, bitterness, and sweetness. But you only need *one bite* of something sweet at the end of a meal to round off the dining experience. You do not need to eat an entire dessert.

Avoid White Flour Products

The third white poison you must avoid is anything that contains *white flour*. This includes breads, rolls, pastries of all kinds, bagels, and doughnuts. Carbohydrates such as potatoes, rice, and pasta will also make you fat.

Whole grain products are different. They are loaded with vitamins, minerals, and first-class proteins. They are exclusively complex carbohydrates. Not only do they satisfy your appetite in small quantities, but they also contain loads of nutrients that give you a feeling of satisfaction and lightness, rather than feeling heavy and full.

In Barry Sears' best selling book, *The Zone* (Regan Books, 1995), he explains that the body is not very good at breaking down white flour products. When you eat them, they form a thick gluten that moves slowly through your digestive system, making you feel sleepy and causing constipation.

Another reason to avoid these foods is that the whiteness in a white flour product is achieved by first of all milling the wheat to a fine consistency and then removing most of the nutrients. What is left over is then bleached, which kills any nutrients remaining. What you end up with in a white flour product is essentially an "inert" food. It is actually dead. It contains no nutritional value whatsoever.

In fact, all you get from consuming a white flour product, like bread, a roll, or a bagel, is a form of simple carbohydrate, containing no vitamins, minerals, or proteins. The very act of eliminating white flour products from your diet will immediately cause you to lose weight, have more energy, feel lighter, and give you greater stamina throughout the day.

Why Many Foods Are Not Good for You

As an exercise, you should look at the "contents list" on the labels of canned or packaged foods sold in your local supermarket. You will be amazed to find that most canned and fast foods are loaded with sugar and salt. Sometimes, sugar or salt is the largest single ingredient in foods like canned soups or soft drinks. Why is this?

The reason has to do with preservation. What food manufactures found very early was that the best way to stop a food from rotting or decomposing on the supermarket shelf was to *kill* the food before you send it to the store in the first place. By immersing a food in salt or sugar, you actually kill it so that it will last much longer on the shelf, or in your pantry. But by killing it, you eliminate most of the food value that it would have if it were fresh.

Develop the habit of organizing your diet around foods that do not contain salt, sugar, or flour. Instead, eat fresh foods, with bright colors, that are high in nutrients. By eating highly nutritious foods, you will begin to lose weight immediately. You will feel lighter and more alert, have more stamina, and function at far higher levels, both mentally and physically.

Timing Is Important

The time you eat during the day is almost as important as what you eat. Nutritionists have found that you need about 2,000 calories per day for ideal functioning. However, when you consume these calories will determine whether or not you gain or lose weight. If you consume 80 percent of your 2,000 calories at breakfast and lunch and only 20 percent of your calories after 2 P.M. you will lose weight steadily. If however, you eat a light breakfast, a light lunch, and then a heavy dinner, consuming 60 to 80 percent of your calories after 2 P.M. you will gain weight eating the same 2,000 calories that someone else is consuming and losing weight.

From now on, resolve to eat as Adele Davis, the diet guru once advised, "Eat breakfast like a king, lunch like a prince, and dinner like a pauper." By disciplining yourself to eat light and lean in the evenings and not to eat anything in the three hours before bedtime, you will sleep better and wake up more refreshed.

Turn Off Your Appestat

Develop the habit of eating half portions, of eating lightly rather than heavily at each meal. Eat better foods, containing more nutrients, and eat fewer of them. Use a smaller plate when you dish out your portions, and stop eating when you are no longer hungry.

Just as a room has a thermostat that keeps the temperature within a certain range, each person has an "appestat" that regulates their appetite. This appestat, which tells you that you are hungry, continues to function for about 20 minutes after you eat the first bite of food. At the end of 20 minutes, your appestat switches off, and your appetite disappears. From then on, you are not eating for nutrition, but for pleasure.

You can turn off your appestat deliberately by beginning a meal with soup, fruits, or vegetables of some kind. By eating and chewing slowly, stretching out the initial part of the meal past the 20-minute point, you can actually kill your appetite, satisfy your hunger, and end up eating less and feeling better. You can actually trick yourself into eating less and losing weight. Even eating something like a piece of fruit or a few nuts will begin the process of shutting down your appestat and enable you to stop eating.

You Become What You Eat

Develop the habit of viewing your body as a chemical factory. You know that you become what you eat. Nutritionists have concluded that everything you put into your body is broken down into its individual chemical components and is then absorbed by your body in the process of digestion.

Before you put anything in your mouth, carefully consider the chemical components of the food. Does this foodstuff contain the particular nutrients that are the very best for you at this time? What we refer to as a "junk food" is a food that is composed of elements containing no nutrients that are simultaneously hard to break down and digest. Junk foods are inert, dead, useless foods that provide nothing except the momentary olfactory and gustatory pleasure experienced at the moment of eating them. Refuse to put junk foods and other poor quality foods into your chemical factory.

Imagine that you became extremely wealthy and were able to purchase an expensive racehorse, one that cost perhaps one million dollars. What kinds of foods would you give to this racehorse? Would you allow this racehorse to eat candy bars, potato chips, bagels, and other high carbohydrate, low-nutrient foods? Of course not!

Think of how much more valuable you are as a person. You are certainly worth more than one million dollars. You should at least treat yourself as well as you would treat an animal you had purchased.

GET LOTS OF EXERCISE

The third habit you need to develop is the habit of proper exercise. Many people who were active in sports when they were growing up stop exercising in their late teens and early 20s. However, the human body, made up of 610 muscles, is meant to be exercised regularly throughout your life.

Develop the habit of articulating and moving every joint in your body every single day. This keeps your muscles and joints agile and flexible. Regular exercise assures that you have greater balance and mobility. It helps to diminish the likelihood of muscle or joint pain or problems.

Develop the habit of exercising 200 minutes each week. If all you do is go for a walk, 30 minutes per day, seven days per week, you would be one of the fittest people in our society. If you disciplined yourself to ride an exercise bicycle, work out on a treadmill, swim, jog, or engage in any aerobic exercises that get your lungs and heart pumping, you will dramatically improve your levels of health and energy in a short period of time.

Many people do not like to exercise. Well, that's too bad. If your goal is to live a long and healthy life, to be slim, trim, and attractive to members of the opposite sex, to have high levels of self-esteem and personal pride, it is absolutely essential that you become physically fit. Fortunately, physical fitness is eminently achievable if you just develop some of the habits I am talking about in this chapter.

TAKE GOOD CARE OF YOURSELF

The next habit you need for superb all-around health is the habit of proper rest. You need seven to eight hours of sleep each night for optimal performance. If you get less than six to seven hours of sleep per night, and you continue to work as hard as you normally do at your job, you will eventually develop a "sleep deficiency."

It is estimated that more than 60 percent of Americans are walking around today in a form of "fog." They are going to bed too late, often after having eaten late as well, sleeping poorly, arising not fully rested, and going through the day without the ability to function at their best, mentally and physically.

You can change the way you feel about yourself and your performance in your work and personal life by developing the habit of going to bed early, by 10 P.M. each night and getting a good night's sleep every night of the week. Many people who have increased their sleeping hours from five or six to seven or eight have been absolutely amazed at the difference. They feel as if they have woken from a deep slumber. They feel brighter and clearer and are more alert, creative, and intelligent. Sufficient rest is really important.

Take Regular Vacations

In my company, Advanced Coaching and Mentoring Program, we teach people to set a goal of taking 120 to 150 days off each year. Initially, our clients are incredulous. They claim it is simply impossible. It cannot be done. They are too busy. They have too much to do. If anything, they need to take off *less* time so they can get caught up with all of their responsibilities.

However, if you develop the habit of taking every weekend off completely, allowing your mental and physical batteries to recharge, that will amount to a total of 104 days per year. If you take off every public holiday, that will be six more days per year, making a total of 110 days. If you take off four, six, or eight weeks each year on vacation, and refuse to do anything associated with work during that time, you will soon be taking off 120 to 150 days each year, almost without noticing it.

As you do this, something extraordinary will happen in your work. You will be brighter and more alert. You will be more intelligent and creative. You will come up with a continuous stream of ideas and insights that will enable you to accomplish vastly more than the people around you.

It seems that the more rest you get and the more rested you are as the result of going to bed early and taking regular vacations, the more productive you become, the fewer mistakes you make, and the faster you move ahead in your career.

I have studied this subject at great length for many years. What I have concluded is that you can take off as many as three full months each year and simultaneously increase your productivity, performance, output, and income. Whenever we teach our clients to do this, they are absolutely astonished at how much more money they make, how much faster they move ahead in their field, and how much better they feel. We have never had an exception to this rule.

Early to Bed and Early to Rise

In addition to the habit of proper rest, develop the habit of going to bed early and arising early. Almost all successful people practice the old saying, "Early to bed and early to rise makes a person healthy, wealthy, and wise."

When you get up early, at 5:30 or 6:00 in the morning, you will have ample time to think about the day ahead and to plan your work activities. Early rising gives you an opportunity to read, reflect, and meditate. Early rising enables you to get up and get going without a feeling of pressure to rush out of the house in order to get to work on time.

Develop the habit of investing the first hour of the day in yourself. Read something inspirational, motivational, or educational. Rewrite and reflect on your goals. Henry Ward Beecher once wrote, "The first hour is the rudder of the day." When you invest this first hour in yourself, the rest of your day will seem much smoother, and will unfold with great efficiency and effectiveness.

Develop the habit of eating an excellent, high protein breakfast with no toast, bacon, or sausage. Eat a high quality lunch, ideally composed of a salad with protein such as chicken or fish. Eat a light dinner, primarily composed of vegetables with a little protein, but no breads, rolls, or pasta. By developing the habit of eating in this way, you will soon have your weight and your health under control.

Drink Lots of Water

In addition to proper weight, diet, exercise, and rest, develop the habit of proper hydration as well. More and more people are finding that the consumption of large quantities of water throughout the day is one of the most important things they can do for excellent health.

The average person sips water throughout the day. But this is not enough. You need approximately two full quarts of water throughout the day to maintain the proper level of hydration in your body. Instead of sipping when you go past the drinking fountain, drink full glasses of water, at least once every hour.

You can tell if you are properly hydrated, rather than dehydrated, by looking at the color of your urine. When you are drinking sufficient quantities of water, your urine will be almost clear. When you are dehydrated, on the other hand, your urine will be a deep yellow and sometimes even brown.

You cannot drink too much water. If you drink any excess, it will just pass through in a short period of time.

Drinking lots of water has several great benefits. The most important is that proper hydration serves the purpose of detoxifying your body continually throughout the day. When you drink lots of water, the water washes away excess salt, sugar, and other toxins that interfere with excellent health and functioning. You feel brighter and more alert. You become more creative and focused. If you are currently overweight, drinking lots of water will wash away the extra salt that often causes you to feel fat and bloated. This washing away of excess salt will cause you to lose weight. You cannot drink too much water.

Take Vitamin and Mineral Supplements

An important health habit for you is the habit of taking vitamin and mineral supplements each day. The fact is, you simply do not get enough of the essential vitamins and minerals you need for optimum health in your current diet. There are a thousand reasons for this, including the excessive use of fertilizers and pesticides in growing crops, the depletion of the soil, and the way that foodstuffs are processed before they get to your table.

However, when you take high quality vitamin and mineral supplements along with your meals, you will be assured of getting all the nutrients you need for high levels of energy and fitness.

One of the arguments against vitamin and mineral supplements is, "You get all the vitamins and minerals you need if you just eat a proper diet."

This may be true, but nutritionists have calculated that you would need to consume about 20 pounds of food per day, including a wide variety of fruits, vegetables, whole grain products, and lean source proteins to get the entire range of vitamins and minerals you require to function at your best. It is much better, easier, and more controllable for you to take vitamin and mineral supplements on a regular basis.

PRACTICE EXCELLENT DENTAL HYGIENE

Develop the habit of brushing and flossing your teeth twice each day. There seems to be a direct relationship between dental health and hygiene and physical health and hygiene. People who take excellent care of their teeth tend to be healthier physically as well. Not only that, they look better, have cleaner, fresher breath, and are more attractive to others.

Get Regular Checkups

Develop the habit of getting regular physical and dental checkups. Today, we have the most advanced medical technology and the best doctors in the history of the world available to us to enable us to live well and live longer. But none of these benefits or advantages will do you any good if you do not get regular checkups.

Many of the life-threatening diseases, such as heart disease and various forms of cancer, can be detected years before they become dangerous if you get regular checkups. It is tragic to learn about friends who died from cancer or heart disease because they put off going to a doctor until it was too late. Don't let this happen to you.

PRACTICE MODERATION IN ALL THINGS

Develop the habit of temperance, or "moderation in all things." Just as you should eat less than your stomach is capable of holding, you should also apply the principle of temperance to other things that you consume as well, especially alcohol.

According to the Alameda Study, covering more than 20,000 men over a 22-year period, one of the most important of all health habits is "moderate to nil alcohol consumption." One of the major killers in our society today is cirrhosis of the liver. Another is the number of people killed in automobile accidents as the result of drunken driving. The practice of temperance, or moderation in alcohol consumption, is an essential habit for long life.

Belt Yourself In

Another discovery of the Alameda Study is the importance of wearing seatbelts when you drive. There is a saying that "they only have to work once."

More than 42,000 people die each year as the result of automobile accidents. Most of these deaths could be avoided if people were wearing full seat and shoulder belts. Make it a habit to fasten your seatbelt whenever you get into your car. Insist that your passengers fasten their seatbelts as well. This will not only give you an edge in terms of long life, it can save the life of your passengers. It is a small effort for a huge potential benefit.

Clean as a Whistle

Develop the habit of cleanliness and excellent hygiene in every part of your life. Bathe and shower regularly, wash your hair, brush your teeth, clean your fingernails, and resolve to look excellent in every respect. Use proper deodorant and mouthwash. Wear clean clothes each day. Not only will you be more attractive to others, but practicing high levels of cleanliness and orderliness in your personal and business life will also improve your self-image and increase your self-esteem.

Researchers have discovered that teachers pay greater attention to students who come to school clean and well dressed than they do to students who come poorly dressed and unkempt. By the same token, bosses, customers, and co-workers are far more likely to be impressed and influenced by people who look and smell good at work. It is a big payoff for a small effort.

BECOME AN UNSHAKABLE OPTIMIST

One of the most important habits you can develop for health, happiness, and long life is the habit of maintaining a positive attitude toward the people and situations in the world around you. Remind yourself of the serenity prayer: "God grant me the ability to change the things I can, the willingness to accept the things I cannot, and the wisdom to know the difference," (Reinhold Niebuhr).

Resolve to maintain a positive mental attitude no matter what happens. Refuse to allow yourself to become upset or angry when people and situations do not measure up to your expectations. Instead, be calm, relaxed, and focused on solutions to the problems and difficulties facing you.

PRACTICE SOLITUDE DAILY

Develop the habit of taking time for yourself, in solitude and meditation each day. Reserve for yourself a 30- to 60-minute period where you can be completely alone, in the silence. Turn off all radio and television, put aside all reading materials, and just allow yourself to commune deeply with the world around you.

Blaise Pascal, the French writer, once wrote, "All the problems in the world originate because of man's inability to be alone in a room with himself."

Most people have never practiced solitude and meditation. We are so busy, with so much to do and so little time, that we feel we cannot take the few minutes necessary to sit quietly and be alone with ourselves. But this is mistaken.

Each time you sit in solitude for 30 minutes or more, you will feel your mind becoming clear and calm. The problems and difficulties facing you will become lighter and easier to bear. You will receive superconscious insights and ideas to deal with the challenges of your day-to-day life. You will arise from a period of solitude greatly refreshed, mentally, emotionally, and spiritually, and with wonderful thoughts about how you can improve the quality of your life and work.

SET PEACE OF MIND AS YOUR MOST IMPORTANT GOAL

Develop the habit of making "peace of mind" your most important goal in life and then organize all of your life and activities around this goal. Listen to your inner voice. Trust your intuition. Only do what feels right and natural for you to do.

When you begin to focus on developing greater peace of mind and listening to your intuition, you will probably never make another mistake. You will always find yourself doing and saying the right things, in the right way, at the right time. As you trust your inner voice, you will receive an endless flow of ideas, insights, and creative solutions to solving your problems and achieving your every goal.

Doctors who have participated in my seminars tell me that fully 85 percent or more of all physical illnesses and ailments today are psychosomatic in origin: "psycho," the mind, makes "soma," the body, sick. The very act of letting go and relaxing and practicing solitude and meditation on a regular basis dramatically lowers your levels of stress and tension and raises your levels of energy and awareness.

The more centered you are within yourself, and the more positive and optimistic your thinking, the healthier and happier you will be, and the longer you will live. By placing peace of mind as the central organizing principle of your life, you will become a more effective, efficient, and happier person. The journey of your life will be far longer than that of the average person, and you will enjoy every step along the way.

Action Exercises

$ Practice future orientation and "idealize" perfect health for yourself. What level of health would you have if you were physically perfect in every respect?

$ Write out a description of your ideal future health, as if you had no limitations and could achieve any condition you desired.

$ Set clear, written, time-bounded goals for your weight, waist size, number of minutes of exercise per week, and physical activities.

Action Exercises, *continued*

$ Make a complete health plan to live to be 100 years old. What would you immediately do more of, or less of, to reach that goal in fine form?

$ Organize your vacation schedule for the next year, in advance, and make the necessary bookings, with deposits, immediately.

$ Determine the one health habit that could help you the most at the moment and then launch into this habit immediately. Allow no exceptions until it is a permanent part of your behavior.

$ Resolve to take time for yourself each day in solitude and meditation, either first thing in the morning or in the evening; keep this appointment with yourself.

A strong, successful man is not the victim of his
environment. He creates favorable conditions. His
own inherent force and energy compel things
to turn out as he desires.

—Orison Swett Marden

12

The Habits of Character and Leadership

> The beauty of the soul shines out when a man
> bears with composure one heavy mischance
> after another, not because he does not
> feel them, but because he is a man
> of high and heroic temper.
>
> —ARISTOTLE

*T*HE ULTIMATE AIM OF HUMAN LIFE AND activity is the development of character, according to Aristotle. The most important goal you could hope to accomplish in the course of your life is to become an excellent person, in every respect. Your purpose should be to develop the kind of personality and character that earns you the respect, esteem, and affection of the important people in your world.

Men and women of great character are those who have developed the habits of thinking and behaving that are consistent with the fine qualities they wish to be known for. They discipline themselves to do the right thing in every situation. By working on themselves and by steady effort, great people in our world, living and dead, have behaved in certain ways whether they felt like it or not.

In his *Nicomachaen Ethics*, Aristotle wrote about the great virtues possessed by the leading men and women of the age. He concluded that each virtue is a "golden mean" between the extremes of that quality on either side. For example, he concluded that courage was the golden mean between cowardliness on the one extreme and impetuosity on the other. He taught that it should be each person's goal in life to reach the golden mean in each virtue, quality, or attribute that he or she aspires to.

THE EDUCATION OF THE YOUNG

Aristotle also wrote, "All improvement in society begins with the education of the young." One of the primary responsibilities of those in charge of educating young people is to instill in them the importance of virtue, character, and good behavior. Children are inordinately influenced by the people around them while they are growing up. This is the time when young people are most capable of incorporating the finest qualities into their characters.

But what if you have reached adulthood without the virtues and qualities you most admire and aspire to? What can you do? Well, fortunately all virtues and values are merely habits of thinking and acting. You can learn any habit you consider to be either desirable or necessary. You can learn a virtue or value of character and leadership the same way you develop a physical skill or habit—by practice and repetition.

DEVELOP YOUR OWN CHARACTER

Aristotle, probably the greatest philosopher and thinker of all time, said a simple method can help, if you wish to learn a virtue later in life. Simply practice the virtue in every situation where that virtue is required. In other words, if you wish to develop the quality of courage, act courageously even when you feel afraid. If you wish to develop the quality of generosity, be generous on every occasion, even if your feel stingy. As you practice and repeat the virtue, it becomes more and more a part of your personality. It soon becomes automatic and easy. Eventually, you will reach the point where you cannot imagine acting in any other way.

Decide today to become a "do-it-to-yourself" project. Establish a series of goals and a work schedule for the development of your own character and personality. Set high standards for yourself and resolve to develop the habits of excellent behavior practiced by the men and women you most admire.

Imagine Your Ideal Self

When we spoke about self-concept in Chapter 1, we talked about the role of the "self-ideal" in shaping and forming personal character. The greater clarity you have about the qualities you most admire and desire to incorporate into your personality, the easier it is for you to engage in behaviors consistent with those virtues and values. The more repeatedly you engage in those behaviors, the more you internalize those qualities, until they become a permanent part of you.

The starting point of character development is for you to develop the habit of long-term thinking in your work and in your personal life. There is no area where this is more relevant than for you to project to the end of your life and write your own eulogy to be read at your funeral where your friends and family are gathered. If you could fulfill your potential and become the very best person that it is possible for you to become, how would people think about you, talk about you, and describe you to others? What words would they use? What virtues, values, and qualities would they ascribe to you? How would you be remembered—and for what reasons?

Acting as If You Were Already That Person

As you develop greater clarity about how you want to be remembered in the hearts and minds of other people, you will become clearer about those values and qualities most important to you. You can then set those qualities as goals for yourself and make plans for their accomplishment. From

Change Your Destiny

Many years ago, the brother of Alfred Nobel died in Stockholm. But the newspapers got the name wrong, concluded it was Alfred Nobel himself who had died, and wrote his obituary, which he read the next day. In Nobel's premature obituary, he was remembered primarily for inventing dynamite, which had been responsible for the deaths of countless human beings in wars and conflicts around the world.

This obituary had such a shocking effect on Nobel that he immediately began rearranging his entire life to change his legacy and assure that his obituary, when it was ultimately written, would be completely different. To this end, he established the Nobel Prizes, based on his great fortune, which are today the highest awards that can be attained in the worlds of literature, medicine, science, economics, peace, and chemistry. By thinking clearly about the legacy he wanted to leave, he transformed both his present actions and his ultimate memory. He rewrote his own obituary.

To become a person of great quality and value, you should develop the habit of reading about and studying about other men and women who have started with little or nothing and who have gone on to accomplish wonderful things with their lives. It seems that many men and women who achieve greatness as adults spend many hours as children reading the biographies and autobiographies of successful people. Because young people are so susceptible to the suggestive influences of others, as they read, they began to envision and imagine themselves having the same qualities as the people that they were reading about. And that is exactly what happened in many cases.

that point forward, you "act as if" you already had those qualities whenever they are called for.

If you wish to develop the quality of *patience*, for example, practice being patient even when you feel pressured or in a hurry. If you wish to develop the quality of compassion, practice putting yourself in the situation of the other person and thinking, "There but for the grace of God, go I."

This habit of projecting yourself forward into the distant future and then looking back to the present for guidance on the steps you should take each day can have a profound impact on your life.

ASPIRE TO LEADERSHIP

It is not easy to rise to a position of leadership in any organization or in any society. The competition for leadership is fierce. Only the people who are the very best equipped to acquire leadership positions and then to hold on to those positions rise to the top in any area.

Different areas of endeavor require different qualities of leadership. The qualities of leadership necessary to direct an army at war are very different from the qualities of leadership necessary to direct a large university. The qualities of leadership necessary to start and build a successful entrepreneurial business are very different from the leadership qualities necessary to run a large organization.

Whatever It Takes

In a way, leadership is "situational." What is necessary for success in a leadership position is determined by many factors, including the people to be led; the objectives to be accomplished; the competition for resources; the social, cultural, political, and economic environment; and the situation that the leader finds at the moment. Changing any one of these factors will change the qualities of leadership necessary for success.

More than 3,300 studies of leadership have been conducted over the years going back as far as 600 B.C. and Thucydides' *History of the Peloponnesian War*, and they point to more than 50 different qualities leaders have or develop over time. Of those qualities, a few seem to be present in almost every leader who accomplishes great things and earns the undying respect, esteem, and loyalty of other people, even long after that leader has passed from the scene. The one quality all these studies on leadership held in common is the quality of "vision." Leaders have vision; ordinary people do not.

Develop a Vision

To become a person of character and a leader in your own life and world, the first habit you must develop is the habit of vision. You must develop the habit of projecting forward several years into the future. You must develop the habit of developing absolute clarity about what you want to accomplish in your position and what it will look like if you are successful.

One way to develop a vision for each part of your life is to wave a magic wand in your mind and imagine you have no limitations on what you can be, have, or do. Create a perfect future ideal image of how your situation would appear if it were perfect in every way. Allow your mind to float freely. Imagine you have no limitations of time, money, resources, or ability. Imagine that everything is possible for you.

Just as you would design your dream house if you had an unlimited budget, take some time to design your "dream future" as if you had unlimited abilities and resources. The greater clarity you have regarding your long-term vision, the easier it is for you to motivate and inspire other people to work with you to make that vision a reality.

Be the Best at What You Do

In business, the most important long-term vision you can have for your organization is to "be the best." Identify a quality of your product or service that is relevant and important to your customers and then focus all the energies and creativity of your organization toward achieving superior performance in that area. Developing the habit of thinking in terms of making your business the very best in your industry is an essential quality of visionary leadership. Without this commitment to excellence, by default organizations and individuals slip into mediocre or merely satisfactory performance.

Dare to Go Forward

The second quality you must develop—the second most common habit of great men, women, and leaders at every level—is the habit of courage. Many people have exciting hopes, dreams, and visions for the future. But only a few people have the courage to take the risks necessary to turn those visions into realities.

The most important part of courage is the willingness to launch, to take action in the direction of your goals and dreams, with no guarantee of success. Courage requires you to take risks with time, money, emotion, and other resources. Courage requires you to accept the possibility of losses, setbacks, obstacles, difficulties, and temporary failure.

It is impossible to succeed without failing. Failure seems to be an indispensable prerequisite for success. You only learn to succeed by failing and then evaluating the reasons for your failure. The faster you fail in a forward direction, the faster you succeed.

The Secret to Success

Thomas J. Watson, founder of IBM, was once asked by the young journalist Arthur Gordon, "Mr. Watson, how can I be more successful faster?"

Watson replied with these profound words, "If you want to succeed faster, you must double your rate of failure. Success lies on the far side of failure."

It seems that you will fail far more times than you succeed. Murphy's Law will apply to every new goal that you attempt: "Whatever can go wrong will go wrong. And of all the things that can go wrong, the worst possible things will go wrong at the worst possible times, and cost the most money."

The first corollary to Murphy's Law is, "Murphy was an optimist."

OVERCOMING YOUR FEARS

The way you develop the habit of courage is by acting courageously whenever courage is called for. Ralph Waldo Emerson once wrote that the most important lesson he learned as a young man was, "In every situation do the thing you fear." He concluded, "If you do the thing you fear, the death of fear is certain."

You develop the habit of courage by moving toward the things you fear. You develop the habit of cowardliness by moving away from or avoiding the things or people you fear. From this day forward, make it a habit to confront your fears, to face your fears, to do the things that you fear, and to deal with the people and situations that make you feel fearful. Each time you face a fear and overcome it, not only does your courage increase but so does your self-esteem and self-respect. You become a stronger and more confident person.

Eventually, by continually doing the things you fear, even when your natural tendency is to avoid them, you will reach the point where you are not really afraid of anything. You will recognize that facing fear is just something leaders do each day, like driving through rush hour traffic. It is unfortunate, but inevitable and unavoidable.

The True Test of the Leader

Peter Drucker says the only event that is inevitable in the life of the leader is the "unexpected crisis." Only when you encounter a setback, an obstacle, a difficulty, or the inevitable crisis, do you demonstrate the kind of person you really are. It is not what you say, wish, hope, or intend that reveals your character. It is only your actions, especially your actions in the face of adversity and possible setbacks or losses.

The Greek stoic philosopher Epictetus once wrote, "Circumstances do not make the man; they merely reveal him to himself."

Develop the habit of asking this question, "What one great thing would I dare to dream, if I knew I could not fail?"

Imagine that you have a magic wand you can wave that will absolutely guarantee success in anything you attempt, large or small, long-term or short-term. What goals would you set for yourself if you were guaranteed of success in any area?

Author Dorothy Brande once wrote, "Act as if it were impossible to fail, and it shall be!"

Develop the habit, from this day forward, of identifying the things you fear may be holding you back and then confronting each one of them until they contain no more fear for you. As actor Glenn Ford, once said, "If you do not do the thing you fear, the fear controls your life."

Put another way, "Leap, and the net will appear." Leap, and build your wings on the way down.

Make it a habit to do the things you fear, and the death of fear is certain. As your level of courage and confidence increases, your fears and doubts will decrease. The more you confront your fears and eliminate them, the stronger and more confident you will feel. Your self-esteem and self-respect will rise. As your fears diminish, you will become more powerful and persuasive. You will move forward like a rushing flood. You will become unstoppable.

YOU ARE RESPONSIBLE

Once you have developed a clear vision for your ideal future and resolved to develop unshakable courage by doing the things you fear, you must develop the habit of accepting complete responsibility for yourself and for every aspect of your life.

Leaders accept responsibility. Followers do not. Leaders refuse to make excuses, while followers hide behind them. Leaders see themselves as the primary creative forces in their own lives. Followers see themselves as victims and spend much of their energies rationalizing, justifying, and explaining away their failure to make progress. The acceptance of complete responsibility is as essential to leadership as is courage.

Emerson once wrote that you could measure the size of a person by looking at the size of the responsibilities he or she is willing to take on. There is a direct relationship between responsibility and a sense of control. The more responsibility you accept, the greater control you take over the various aspects of your life. When you accept total responsibility, you feel completely in control of yourself and everything that is happening around you.

Take Charge of Your Emotions

Make it a habit to continually repeat to yourself the words, "I am responsible!" Whenever you feel angry or frustrated about some person or situation, immediately cancel this thought and feeling by saying, "I am responsible!"

Emotionally, it is impossible to accept responsibility and remain angry. When you accept responsibility, you relax and your mind clears. You become more focused and effective. When you take complete responsibility, like putting both hands on the wheel of your own life, you feel in charge. You feel like a master of your own destiny. The habit of taking responsibility unlocks your mental powers and makes you a more positive and optimistic person. It characterizes you as a true leader.

Tell the Truth

Perhaps the most important quality of leadership is the habit of integrity. You develop integrity and become a completely honest person by practicing telling the truth to yourself and others in every situation. Shakespeare wrote, "To thine own self be true, and it must follow, as the night the day, thou cans't not be false to any man."

The most important asset you develop through life is your reputation, and the quality of your reputation is determined by your level of integrity. Shakespeare also wrote, "Who steals my purse steals trash . . . but he that filches from me my good name . . . makes me poor indeed." You must guard your integrity as a sacred thing, as the most important statement about you.

In every part of business and society today, the first quality looked for in an employee, a manager, a chief executive, and even a friend or spouse is honesty. You must develop the habit of living in truth with yourself and with everyone around you. This does not mean you will always be right, but you will always endeavor to tell the truth as you see it. People will know that they can always rely on you and your word. They may not like what you say, but they will know that you always speak the truth. This is one of the very best reputations you can possibly earn.

Decide What You Stand For

Living in truth means that you live consistent with the highest values that you know. This requires that you develop the habit of thinking through who you are and what you believe in. You continually clarify what you stand for and what you will not stand for. Once you have decided that you are going to build your life around certain values, you refuse to compromise those values for anything.

A client of mine once explained integrity with these profound words, "Integrity is not so much a value as it is the value that guarantees all the other values."

This is a wonderful insight. When you set integrity as your highest value, it becomes much easier for you to make decisions in each area of your life. You simply ask yourself, "Is this consistent with the very best that I know?"

If it is not, you refuse to do it. General Norman Schwarzkopf, commander of U.S. forces during the 1991 Gulf War, once said the most important leadership principle he had learned was simply, "Do the right thing."

Whenever you are in doubt about a course of action, simply ask yourself, "Is this the right thing to do?" And then behave accordingly.

BE A ROLE MODEL FOR OTHERS

The men and women—living and dead—who are the most admired, esteemed, and respected in our society are those who live or lived lives of exemplary honesty and integrity in everything they did. They were absolutely trustworthy. They always told the truth. You could always count on them and believe in them.

George Washington is often called the "father of his country." It was said that America only came into being because of the incredible character of George Washington. It was the respect that the founding fathers had for the honesty and integrity of Washington that held them together during the darkest days of the Revolutionary War.

Abraham Lincoln, considered the second most important and esteemed president in American history, got the nickname of "Honest Abe" as a young man when he walked several miles to return a few pennies to a woman who had overpaid at the general store where he was working. Throughout his career, Lincoln was esteemed and respected as one of the most honest men of his day. This is a wonderful reputation for you to have as well.

The Three Primary Virtues

Adam Smith, in his important book *The Theory of Moral Sentiments*, wrote that excellent people have three primary virtues: prudence, justice, and benevolence, in that order. Each of them is essential to the others and to the living of a full life in society.

PRUDENCE

The virtue of prudence refers to your developing the habit of providing well for yourself, your family, your friends, your co-workers, and your company. This requires that you think intelligently and honestly about the very best course of action to maximize your opportunities and minimize possible danger and threats. The habit of prudence means you investigate every investment carefully, think ahead about what might happen if you were to take a particular course of action, and take intelligent steps to guard against setbacks and reversals of fortune.

The most successful people are those who are prudent in the conduct in all of their personal and business affairs.

JUSTICE IS BLIND

The second habit for you to develop is the habit of justice. This refers to your commitment to the establishment and maintenance of laws in society that protect the person and property of every individual. The American republic has endured for more than 200 years because it was carefully established by the founding fathers on the basis of law, not men. At every level of our society, specific laws are prescribed and laid down that are applicable to all people, regardless of wealth or station in life.

John Rawls, the Harvard philosopher and author of *A Theory of Justice* (Belknap Press, revised edition, 1999), once presented a question to his class that has been repeated often through the years.

Imagine that you could write the laws and create the circumstances of your society. You are given the power to prescribe the economic, social and political relationships that would exist in your country throughout your lifetime.

There is only one limitation on your power. You would set up this structure without knowing into what sort of family or situation you would be born. You would not know in advance what sort of physical condition you might be born with. Whatever system of laws and customs you decided upon, you would then be required to live under them for the rest of your life. What kind of structure would you design in this situation?

The answer to this question is the very essence of the concept of justice. The statue of justice, holding the balances and scales in her hand, is blindfolded. True justice is therefore applicable to all people who live under a certain system, irrespective of their background. When you make the habit of justice an organizing virtue for your own character, you will insist that, whatever the relative power of the parties, everyone be treated fairly and justly in the resolution of any difficulty or dispute.

The habit of prudence is essential for personal success. The habit of justice is essential for the creation of a society within which a person can pursue his or her own best interests with the greatest of possibilities. The rule is that you should never want or demand anything for anyone else that you are not perfectly willing to accept for yourself.

BENEVOLENCE

The third quality you must develop is the habit of benevolence. This is one of the hallmark characteristics of the truly superior person. Aristotle referred to it as one of the eight essential virtues, that of "generosity."

Most people are psychologically and emotionally structured in such a way that they are only truly happy and satisfied when they feel they are doing something that serves and benefits other people. When you give freely and generously of yourself to others, whether it is to members of your family or to members of the public, you feel more valuable and happier inside. When you dedicate yourself to serving your customers with the very best quality product or service of which you are capable, not only do you feel a deep sense of personal satisfaction but you also put yourself on the side of the angels when it comes to personal and business success.

You remember the principle: "The more you give of yourself to others without expectation of return, the more good things there are that will come back to you from the most unexpected sources."

The regular practice of prudence, justice, and benevolence leads naturally to feelings and actions of kindness, compassion, and tolerance toward other people. You become more open minded and flexible. You develop greater patience and understanding. You are less judgmental or demanding of others. You become a better and finer person.

BELIEVE IN SOMETHING GREATER

One of the most important habits you can develop is the habit of faith. Regardless of your religious or spiritual beliefs, it seems that most great men and women are men and women of faith, to a high degree.

By faith, I don't mean that you believe in a dogmatic and inflexible set of religious principles or doctrines. The habit of faith requires that you simply believe that there is a higher power in the universe and that this power wants the very best for you. The greater faith you develop, the greater confidence you will have that everything that is happening to you is part of a great plan that is moving you inevitably toward something better.

Seek the Valuable Lesson

When you have faith, you believe that every setback contains a lesson that has been sent to you to help you. Norman Vincent Peale used to say, "When God wants to send you a gift, He wraps it up in a problem. The bigger the problem He wraps it up in, the bigger the gift that it contains."

Most people are so preoccupied with the problem, difficulty, or obstacle that they neglect to look inside of it for the gift that it might contain. One of the most important habits you can ever develop is an unshakable belief that every problem in your experience has been sent to you at exactly the right moment in your life to teach you something you need to know to be more successful and happier in the future.

Author Napoleon Hill once wrote, "Within every difficulty or obstacle is contained the seed of an equal or greater benefit or advantage."

The more you search for the benefit or advantage, for the valuable lesson or insight, the more likely it is that you will find it. Sometimes, your whole life will be changed as the result of a lesson you learn from an unexpected reversal of fortune or temporary failure.

Your ability to develop and maintain the habit of faith clears your mind, gives you greater self-confidence, and enables you to tune into a higher power that will then guide you to always do and say the right thing at the right time.

LOYALTY IS ESSENTIAL

The habit of loyalty seems to be a quality of the very best people in our society. Disloyalty is a major reason for failure in business and the world of work. The decision from the outset that you will be completely loyal to the people who expect and deserve your loyalty enables you to remain clear and focused in the face of short-term successes and reversals.

Some time ago, one of the Big Three Automakers in Detroit arranged a public demonstration against Japanese imports, demanding quotas, restrictions and higher tariffs in order to protect American manufacturing and jobs. As they had been ordered, the automobile workers arrived for the demonstration from all over Detroit. To the surprise and chagrin of the organizers, many of the Detroit autoworkers were driving Japanese cars. These workers were not even prepared to buy the same cars they were manufacturing, a fact that became a source of major embarrassment when the television crews began filming the arriving demonstrators.

Support Your Family, Friends, and Company

The habit of loyalty requires that you be absolutely loyal to your company. You never criticize your boss or the people you work with, especially outside the company. In addition, you purchase and use the products and services of your company, and recommend them proudly to others. It is amazing how many people work for one company but use the products and services of a competitor. They are then amazed to find that they are seldom, if ever, promoted to positions of higher responsibility. Their disloyalty disqualifies them from any kind of advancement.

It is essential that you be completely loyal to your spouse and to your children. When I was growing up, my parents, as a result of their own difficult upbringings, would turn on their children, including myself, at the slightest complaint or criticism from a neighbor or a teacher. No matter what was said about us by others, our parents would always take the side of the other person and assume that we were guilty before hearing our explanation of what had happened.

LEARN FROM EXPERIENCE

This young experience taught me something that has been priceless in my own personal life. From the birth of my first child, I have devoted myself to practicing 100 percent unconditional loyalty to my children, no matter what mistakes they made or what trouble they got into (and all children get into things when they are growing up).

Probably in reaction to my childhood, I have been strongly loyal to my friends and business associates throughout my life as well. Once I have decided that a person is my friend or colleague, I will stand by them almost indefinitely. I will praise them to others and defend them if they are attacked. I will take any challenge to the character or personality of a friend or relative as if it were a personal attack on me. You should do the same.

NEVER GIVE UP

Another quality of character and leadership that seems to be indispensable for great success is the habit of persistence and determination. Napoleon Hill wrote, "Persistence is to the character of man as carbon is to steel."

Earlier in this book, I explained the Law of Belief and the fact that your deeply held beliefs become your realities. You always act in a manner consistent with the way you believe inside, your self-concept. In my estimation, your level of persistence is the true measure of your belief in yourself and your ability to succeed.

Imagine that there was a "belief store" just like a "computer store" in your neighborhood. You could go down to this belief store and buy a belief and program it into your subconscious mind, just as you would load a new computer program onto your hard drive. If this were the case and you could buy any belief that you wanted, what would be the best belief for you to purchase to program into your subconscious mind?

In Napolean Hill's interviews with more than 500 successful men and women, he found they all had one particular belief in common. Each of them absolutely believed they were destined to be great successes in life. They believed that everything that was happening to them in the short term was part of a great plan to ultimately make them successful. They held to this belief through every storm of life. It eventually became unshakable. They saw the world in terms of inevitable success and personal greatness. And as a result, their beliefs became true. Each of these great men and women went on to accomplish wonderful things with their lives.

The Big Payoff

The good news is that the more you persist in the face of disappointment, disillusionment, setbacks, obstacles, and temporary failure, the stronger you become as a person. The more you persist, the more you come to believe in yourself. And the more you believe in yourself, the more you will persist, no matter what happens. Each of them, persistence and belief, reinforces the other until you ultimately become unstoppable.

Earlier in this book, I emphasized the importance of self-discipline in developing the habits that lead you on to happiness, health, and great achievement. The truth is that persistence is self-discipline in action. Each time you discipline yourself to persist, especially when you feel like quitting, both your ability to discipline yourself in subsequent events and your strength of persistence increases. Each reinforces the other.

We know that your level of self-esteem—how much you like and respect yourself—lies at the core of your personality. How much you like yourself determines how positive and optimistic you are, how resilient you are in the face of adversity, the size of the goals you set for yourself, how well you get along with other people, how healthy you are, and almost everything that happens to you in your work and personal life. Self-esteem is the key to great personal success.

As it happens, each time you discipline yourself to persist in the face of adversity, your self-esteem goes up. You like and respect yourself even more. You become stronger and more determined. You become happier and more confident. Every act of self-discipline reinforces every subsequent act of self-discipline. Every act of persistence reinforces every subsequent requirement for persistence. Every act of persistence and self-discipline builds your self-esteem, makes you stronger, and makes you even more capable of disciplining yourself to persist in the future. All three work together to develop within you the kind of character that makes you a leader in everything you do, and wherever you go.

AN ATTITUDE OF GRATITUDE

The final habit for you to develop in becoming a truly excellent person is the habit of practicing an "attitude of gratitude" in every part of your life. We spoke about this attitude earlier regarding getting along well with others. As a part of character development, it means something more.

The habit of feeling and expressing gratitude, of saying "thank you" to people, and "thank you" to life in general, for all of the things in your life that you should be grateful for, has a wonderful effect on your personality.

An attitude of gratitude makes you a warmer, friendlier, and more genial person. An attitude of gratitude causes you to be more sensitive and aware of people around you and your environment. An attitude of gratitude gives you a great sense of happiness and inner satisfaction. The more gratitude you have, the more gratitude you express, the better and more positive is your personality, the higher is your self-esteem, and the more popular and liked you are by all the people around you.

Be Thankful for Everything

Even in the midst of the greatest difficulties you will experience, you can find things for which you are truly grateful. In fact, if you take a piece of paper and begin to write down the parts of your life for which you should be grateful, you will be amazed at how many items appear on your list.

Think about your physical body. No matter what your condition, you can be grateful for all of your senses, for the miracles of sight, sound, touch, taste, smell, and feeling. You can be thankful for the functioning of your body and for the health of your limbs. You can be grateful for the incredible gift of the life that you have lived up until now, and the great life that lies ahead of you. Just sitting alone in your room, thinking about your current blessings, can give you a page full of reasons to be truly grateful.

Look at your personal life. When you begin making a list of every person in your life and the good qualities and actions of those people, you cannot help but be grateful. Think of every material item in your world, your home, car, clothes, and other possessions, and you will not know where to stop. Just thinking about the health and well-being of the people you care about, your spouse, children and friends, and the qualities of their personalities, will fill a list that goes on and on.

Think of the wonderful experiences you've had in the past, the lessons you've learned, the books you've read, the movies you've seen, the songs you've heard, and the foods you've eaten. Think of the places that you have visited and the experiences that you have had in your travels and work. Look back over the years that have passed and look at the years ahead. Think about the opportunities you have lying ahead of you, and you will be amazed at how many things you have in your life for which you can be truly grateful.

Your Great Good Fortune

The most successful people I have met, including millionaires, multimillionaires, and even billionaires, always seem to describe their successes in life by saying, "Life has been very good to me. I have been so fortunate. I have so many things to be grateful for."

Virtually every successful person I have met attributes their success to other people, to their spouses, their children, their parents, their co-workers, their friends, associates, and customers. Sir Isaac Newton, who is ranked as one of the ten most important people in human history, in the latter years of his life was asked, "How is it that you, amongst all men, could have made so many great contributions to so many sciences?"

Newton replied, thinking of all the great scientists who had preceded him and who worked for so many years before he came along, "If I have seen further . . . it is by standing upon the shoulders of giants."

THE PERSON YOU ARE

Perhaps the greatest breakthrough thought in my life was the discovery that all of us are where we are, and what we are, because of ourselves. We are where we are and what we are because of our habitual thoughts and actions. Men and women of great character, competence, and leadership abilities are those who have worked on themselves, usually for many years, to become the kind of people that others look up to, respect, and admire. They are, in every respect of the word, "self-made" people.

William James of Harvard once wrote, "The greatest revolution of my generation is the discovery that individuals, by changing the inner attitudes of their minds, can change the outer aspects of their lives."

When you go to work on yourself and practice the behaviors you wish to incorporate into your personality and character, you change the inner attitudes of your mind. As a result, you change the outer aspects of your life. You take complete control of your future. You become the very best person you can imagine becoming. There are no limits.

Action Exercises

$ What quality do you admire most in other people? How could you develop this quality in yourself?

$ Imagine that you could write your own eulogy. How would you like to be remembered and described by others when you are gone?

Action Exercises, continued

$ Create a vision for your ideal future. If you could wave a magic wand and make your life ideal in every way, what would it look like?

$ What would you do differently—how would you change your life—if you had no fears at all?

$ Imagine yourself to be a person of complete honesty and impeccable integrity. Is there any behavior of yours that you would change?

$ How would you change your goals and actions if you learned that you had been guaranteed of great success sometime in the future?

$ Resolve today to become a great man or woman, and then practice the habits and behaviors you would have if you were already that person.

Fame is a vapor, popularity an accident, riches
take wings, those who cheer today will curse
tomorrow; only one thing endures—character.

—HORACE GREELEY

About the Author

BRIAN TRACY—KEYNOTE SPEAKER,
CONSULTANT, AND SEMINAR LEADER

Brian Tracy is a successful businessman and one of the top professional speakers in the world. He has started, built, managed, or turned around 22 different businesses. He addresses more than 250,000 people each year throughout the United States, Canada, Europe, Australia, and Asia.

Brian's keynote speeches, talks, and seminars are customized and tailored for each audience. They are described as "inspiring, entertaining, informative, and motivational." He has worked with more than 500 corporations, given more than 2,000 talks, and addressed over 2,000,000 people.

Some of his talks and seminars include:

- **Leadership in the New Millennium.** How to be a more effective leader in every area of business life. Learn the most powerful, practical leadership strategies ever discovered to manage, motivate, and get better results than ever before.
- **21st Century Thinking.** How to outthink, outplan, and outperform your competition. Learn how to get superior results in a fast-moving, fast-changing business environment.
- **The Psychology of Peak Performance.** How the top people think and act in every area of personal and business life. You learn a series

of practical, proven methods and strategies for maximum achievement.

- **Superior Sales Strategies.** How to sell more, faster, and easier to demanding customers in highly competitive markets. Learn how to sell higher-priced products and services against lower-priced competitors.

Brian will carefully customize his talk for you and your audience. Call today for full information on booking Brian to speak at your next meeting or conference. Visit www.briantracy.com, phone (858) 481-2977, or write Brian Tracy International, 462 Stevens Avenue, Suite 202, Solana Beach, CA 92075.

Focal Point Advanced Coaching and Mentoring Program

This intensive one-year program is ideal for ambitious, successful men and women who want to achieve better results and greater balance in their lives.

If you are already earning more than $100,000 per year and if you have a large degree of control over your time, in four full days with me in San Diego—one day every three months—you will learn how to double your productivity and income and double your time off with your family at the same time.

Every 90 days, you work with me and an elite group of successful entrepreneurs, self-employed professionals, and top salespeople for an entire day. During this time together, you form a "mastermind alliance" from which you gain ideas and insights that you can apply immediately to your work and personal life.

The Focal Point Advanced Coaching and Mentoring Program is based on four areas of effectiveness: **Clarification, Simplification, Maximization, and Multiplication.** You learn a series of methods and strategies to incorporate these principles into everything you do.

Clarification. You learn how to develop absolute clarity about who you really are and what you really want in each of seven key areas of life.

You determine your values, vision, mission, purpose, and goals for yourself, your family, and your work.

Simplification. You learn how to dramatically simplify your life, getting rid of all the little tasks and activities that contribute little to the achievement of your real goals of high income, excellent family relationships, superb health and fitness, and financial independence. You learn how to streamline, delegate, outsource, minimize, and eliminate all those activities that are of little value.

Maximization. You learn how to get the very most out of yourself by implementing the best time and personal management tools and techniques. You learn how to get more done in less time, how to increase your income rapidly, and how to have even more time for your personal life.

Multiplication. You learn how to leverage your special strengths to accomplish vastly more than you could by relying on your own efforts and resources. You learn how to use other people's money, other people's efforts, other people's ideas, and other people's customers and contacts to increase your personal productivity and earn more money.

Brian Tracy gives the Focal Point Advanced Coaching and Mentoring Program personally four times each year in San Diego. Each session includes complete pre-work, detailed exercises, and instruction, all materials, plus meals and refreshments during the day. At the end of each session, you emerge with a complete blueprint for the next 90 days.

If you are interested in attending this program, visit our Web site at www.briantracy.com, or phone our Vice President, Victor Risling at 1-800-542-4252 (ext. 17) to request an application form or more information. We look forward to hearing from you.

Index